COMPLETE TRAINING FOR THE
WORKING SPANIEL

COMPLETE TRAINING FOR THE
WORKING SPANIEL

GRAHAM GIBSON

THE CROWOOD PRESS

First published in 2015 by
The Crowood Press Ltd
Ramsbury, Marlborough
Wiltshire SN8 2HR

enquiries@crowood.com

www.crowood.com

This impression 2020

© Graham Gibson 2015

British Library Cataloguing-in-Publication Data
A catalogue record for this book is available from the British Library.

ISBN 978 1 84797 945 2

Acknowledgements
I would never have completed this book without the help of many people. First and foremost, I would like to thank my best friend and partner, Holly S. Donaldson, as without her help and infinite patience, as well as her skill in photography, the book would never have been finished. I would also particularly like to thank Billy Steel Jr and family, and their puppy Shadow; Virginia Colley for her artwork; and a sincere thank-you to everyone else who helped in whatever way to make this book possible.

Thanks are also due to my long-suffering red Cocker Spaniel Willow, who appears in many of the photographs in this book. She has proved invaluable in illustrating the various training methods that she had to perform repeatedly for the camera!

Dedication
I would like to dedicate this book to my son Craig Gibson, who is also a gamekeeper, in the hope that he one day might read it and learn something.

Typeset by Jean Cussons Typesetting, Diss Norfolk
Printed and bound in India by Parksons Graphics

CONTENTS

INTRODUCTION

I was born in the industrial heartland of Scotland in the late fifties. My father worked as a wages clerk for the Distillers Company Ltd and my mother was fully employed raising my brother and I in a small tenement flat in Coatbridge (when she could catch us). My first memory of any kind of 'field sport' was just after the town council decided to fill in the West End Canal, which ran right alongside our tenement. The rats vacated the canal in their thousands, setting up residence in the relative comfort of our communal back yards, wash houses and outside toilets. My mother, her friends and neighbours were horrified, but my brother and I devised every possible method of trying to catch the rats. The hunting instinct must have kicked in because ever since then I have enjoyed every kind of hunting, shooting or fishing.

School was not a happy time for me. Fortunately, I made a few like-minded friends who also much preferred fishing, bird nesting and hunting water rats to sitting in a classroom listening to a teacher. Hence truancy became common and I was an expert at it. Our little group of anglers and hunters spent hours learning the ways of the countryside around West End Park and Coatbridge Lochs, now known as Coatbridge Country Park. We were punished with the belt for non-attendance, and it happened so frequently that eventually my hands and arms became too painful and I just did not go back to school.

Instead I applied for every gamekeeping job I saw advertised – which, in hindsight, were very few (actually none, especially in industrial Coatbridge). However, a very helpful careers adviser managed to get me an interview for a greenkeeper's job, which I dutifully attended, despite not really knowing what a greenkeeper was. I was mortified to learn that I had to cut grass every day and make sure there were no divots missing. I eventually started work as an apprentice earth moving equipment engineer – basically a digger mechanic.

I served my four years' apprenticeship and qualified – not with flying colours, but qualified none the less. It was during this time that I bought my first shotgun. It was a Baikal 32-inch single barrel, which I bought from my mother's catalogue for the princely sum of £17.75, payable in twelve monthly instalments. By this time our family had moved home. My father bought a new house on the outskirts of the city, where we had access to miles upon miles of countryside and unlimited hunting, shooting and helping ourselves to whatever game or rabbits that were available.

I realized that a dog would offer a great advantage, flushing rabbits and retrieving any game that I missed. I could always blame the useless dog... A trip to the pound ensued and for the princely sum of £4 I bought Glen, a Collie-type mongrel. He turned out to be a fantastic dog for flushing rabbits and always seemed to chase them in my direction, allowing for a shot. Unfortunately, he would not retrieve. He would find the dead rabbit and stand over it, but would never demean himself by putting it in his mouth. And he had one major fault: he would severely bite anyone he took exception to. Eventually we had to have him put down before he could do any serious damage. I was heart-broken, but the seed had been sown.

My next encounter with working dogs came when I met Tom McLean, known locally as 'Big Tam', who owned a brown and white Lurcher bitch called Sheena. Short-haired, and looking very much like a greyhound to my inexperienced eye, Sheena was a fantastic dog. She could catch brown hares, mountain hares and foxes, and – even better – retrieve them to hand. I promptly bought two Lurchers, young dogs called Biff and Emma, and proceeded to train them to the best of my ability. We spent the next ten years or so hunting hares, rabbits and foxes. By this time I had a couple of good working terriers to add to my pack, and foxes in my area were beginning to find survival quite a difficult option.

The need for work and responsibility was now seriously interfering with my sport. Luckily, during a fishing trip to Pool Ewe, I met Dougie Russell, who remains a stalker on a large remote estate on Wester Ross. Dougie happened to mention that he employed seasonal ghillies, using only ponies and traditional methods, to bring down from the hills the deer that had been shot by the guests. This sounded like the perfect job for me. Within the week I handed in my notice to my employer, and disappeared into the biggest wilderness tract in Europe for five months, my first full-time job in the sporting world.

One of my Lurchers, Biff, was a real character, but he would not chase deer either roe or red. He treated them much as he would sheep, not for chasing. One day Dougie and I shot seven hinds from a large herd of deer on Chesighan Mhor, one of the highest peaks on our beat. To our dismay, we could not find any of the carcasses. The heather was very long and it was on very steep ground. As usual, I had left Biff asleep next to the ponies, probably around half a mile away. After fifteen minutes or so of futile searching, I whistled for Biff. Amazingly, he found all seven deer within a few minutes. It transpired that we had been searching too high up the hill.

This was a defining moment for me as I then understood just how useful a dog can be. Its much superior sense of smell, coupled with its intelligence and speed, can never be replicated by man or machines. I realized that harnessing the dog's superior abilities and senses to use to our advantage through training and practice would make our working lives much easier.

During my time in the Highlands of Scotland I applied for a few permanent jobs and was lucky enough to start work as a part-time gamekeeper here in Lamington, where I live and work to this day. I was required to have a proper gundog, so made some enquiries through some people I knew who trialled Labradors and subsequently I acquired a one-year-old male Labrador called Kyle – and a book on how to train a gundog. I trained Kyle just as it said in the book and after a few months I was quite proud of my achievement. When Kyle's original owner came down to Lamington to shoot rabbits and do some dog training, he asked to see the dog and enquired how was I getting along with his training. Keen to show off my new dog, I gave him a demonstration, and he suggested that I enter him in a few trials, which I did. As it turned out, we won the first novice trial that we competed in.

At no time in my life did I ever make the decision that I wanted to become a professional dog trainer – it just seemed to happen. After running Kyle in a few trials, I trained more Labradors, ran them for a season and then sold them on. I also ran German Shorthaired Pointers and Spaniels, and subsequently sold them on too. Meanwhile, various people asked me to train their dogs for them. It was at around this time that I decided to build kennels and run them properly as a business in conjunction with my part-time job as a gamekeeper. That was nearly twenty years ago, and since then I have probably trained every conceivable breed, crossbreed and mongrel in basic obedience, as well as training gundogs.

I enjoy my job immensely and thoroughly appreciate how lucky I am to live in such an idyllic part of the country, doing a job that I love. I wouldn't change it for the world. I am writing this book, not only to impart some of my experience and knowledge, but also because I am tired of being known locally as 'that dog trainer guy who lives up in the woods'. Much more prestigious to be known as 'that author guy who lives up in the woods' – don't you think?

Enjoy the book!

CHAPTER 1

CHOOSING A SPANIEL

There are many different types of gundog available in the UK. I often hear from prospective owners who have taken up shooting as a sport and, quite rightly, want to own a gundog. Owning a trained gundog doubles the enjoyment of shooting and there is nothing more rewarding than your dog hunting up a bird or rabbit for you to shoot, then having the satisfaction of your dog retrieving it to hand on command. In fact, I would go so far as to say that shooting without a dog available to retrieve possibly wounded game is morally wrong. If you are willing to shoot a bird, then it is your duty to find it and despatch it humanely if necessary. Without a dog, this is not always possible.

Sometimes the shooter and prospective owner, after having seen perhaps a Weimaraner or Italian Spinone, or some other exotic gundog breed, decides 'that's the dog for me'. While there are some fantastic examples of these breeds that are well trained and do the job we require of them to a very high standard, the vast majority of them are badly or not trained at all, and are a liability to have on a shoot. On the whole they are not dogs for a novice trainer. I am not denigrating these various breeds as gundogs. Probably the finest gundog I have ever seen was a German Shorthaired pointer called Heidi, who was owned and trained by Mr Tommy Brechney; I had one of Heidi's pups, who also turned out to be a fantastic animal, and went on to win an Open Field trial when he was two years old.

There is nothing more satisfying than your Spaniel flushing a bird, you shooting it and your dog retrieving it.

A Brittany Spaniel pointing a covey of grouse. The Brittany is one of the Hunt, Point, Retrieve (HPR) breeds, which on the whole are not for novice trainers.

When I am asked for my opinion on what type of dog to buy, my answer is always that the most common types of dog seen on shoots in the UK are Labradors and Spaniels, simply because as breeds they are perfectly suited to the type of shooting in which we participate. Unlike many other countries, our shooting days are usually social occasions with many people involved, including guns, pickers-up and beaters, and most will have dogs of some description; even on small rough shoots there may be six or seven people out to enjoy the day's sport with their dogs.

TEMPERAMENT

The first and most important factor in the make-up of our gundogs is temperament. In this as a general rule Labradors and Spaniels will not be beaten. There is no place on a shoot for dogs showing aggression to other dogs or to people; indeed, dogs showing this tendency should be discarded and never bred from. The other important temperament traits are natural ability and trainability. We cannot teach our dogs natural ability: this has been built into them over generations by breeding from dogs that excel in the traits we require and discarding from our breeding programmes dogs that do not. This is also the case for trainability. It is useless to have a hard hunting dog and a fantastic retriever if the handler is not in control of the animal; chaos is the only outcome when the dog takes off into the next drive, chasing a bird that was shot at and missed. Invariably the gamekeeper will ask the owner of such a dog to put it on a leash and keep it there, or in the worst scenario will tell them to leave and not come back.

A well trained dog is a major asset to any shoot, while a badly trained one invariably causes trouble and is best left at home.

Labradors and Spaniels are the most common breeds seen at shoots in the UK because they are perfectly suited to our requirements.

A Shoot Day is a social event attracting guns, handlers and dogs.

SPANIEL OR RETRIEVER?

When deciding whether to have a Spaniel or a Retriever, first ask yourself what type of shooting you are mainly involved in. If for most of the time you are a standing gun at driven shoots with almost no time spent hunting up game or in the beating line, then the Retriever breeds are without doubt most suitable for you. The Retriever breeds also excel when it comes to spending hours on the foreshore hunting wild fowl or sitting in a hide decoying pigeons as their heavier build and thicker coat help to retain body heat. Spaniels tend to be more active little dogs, who much prefer to be out there doing something; they are not suited to spending hours in freezing and wet conditions, and they can suffer badly from cold.

Spaniels can suffer badly from the cold.

THE SPANIEL

Most sportsmen, myself included, are involved in various activities related to shooting. For a few days driven shooting, or to walk a drive, stand a drive, rough shooting and walked-up days, or a bit of duck and pigeon shooting with many days picking up or in the beating line, one of the Spaniel breeds would be an excellent choice. The most common of these are the English Springer Spaniel and the Cocker Spaniel simply because they are so well suited to the job, being easily managed and relatively easy to train, and have outstanding energy and stamina. Spaniels have been bred for generations to do exactly these jobs. The Spaniel is a jack of all trades but can be trained to such a high standard that its retrieving ability is on par with any of the Retriever breeds, in addition to its main task of finding and flushing game for the sportsman to shoot.

Working Springer Spaniel.

Cocker Spaniel or English Springer Spaniel?

The choice is down to personal preference; they are bred to do the same job and they both do it well. However, personally I find as breeds there are a few subtle differences which I will try to describe. Firstly, the trainer cannot force a Cocker Spaniel to do something the dog doesn't want to do; with such a dog, the best way is to think around the problem and try a different

Working Cocker Spaniel.

Cocker on the line of a wounded bird.

approach. In contrast, the Springer Spaniel tends to be more straightforward to train and can take a 'telling off'. Secondly, if allowed to, the Cocker can become quite independent of the handler and very quickly ends up hunting for himself rather than hunting for the handler. Having said that, there is no gundog that can surpass a Cocker Spaniel on picking a lightly wing-tipped runner; when he gets on the line of the wounded bird he will stick with it no matter how far the bird runs. Only last season I watched my own Cocker bitch, while working with four of my Springers, take the line of a wounded bird, which had been shot by a guest earlier during the drive, nearly quarter of a mile along the edge of a grouse moor before flipping the bird up and retrieving it. The Springers on this occasion completely failed to acknowledge the scent of the fall. On the whole I find Springers more straightforward to train, and once trained they tend to stay trained, whereas Cockers have to be 'topped up' regularly to keep them in line. The choice is yours.

ACQUIRING A SPANIEL PUPPY

It should be mentioned at this point that there are two distinctly different types of both Cocker and Springer Spaniels: namely working types and show types. In my opinion, if the dog is for working then it is imperative that the buyer chooses a dog with mainly field trial and working lines in its pedigree. They are a completely different type from the show Spaniel, which has been selectively bred for looks alone, to the detriment of any natural ability, trainability and stamina, which are the main traits we require in a working Spaniel. Show dogs tend to be much larger in comparison and, although they can be trained to a degree, they tend to lack any flair for work and are relatively difficult to train. In short, you need a dog that can do the job you want him to do: you would not buy a cart-horse to race in the Grand National, nor buy a racehorse to pull a cart. Make sure your puppy comes from working field trial lines. There are no guarantees that your puppy will turn out to be a useful gundog, although his chances are greatly increased if you buy from the correct working stock.

The best place to start your search for a puppy is without doubt to contact a professional trainer or a successful field trialler and enquire if they know of any suitable litters that are available or forthcoming. Your puppy does not have to be bred from all field trial champion stock, but a few field trial winners or champions in the pedigree will help to ensure that he has the correct blood lines, thus giving you the best chance of success. When you have located a litter and spoken to the owner of the bitch, ask to see her with her pups; find out what she's like and also what the sire is like. You may be able to contact the owner of the sire and arrange to see the sire working. At this stage you are looking at the build and temperament of the parents.

TOP LEFT: Working Cocker Spaniel.

TOP: Show Cocker Spaniel. (Photo: Helen Macleay)

BOTTOM LEFT: Working Springer Spaniel.

RIGHT: Show Springer Spaniel. (Photo: Helen Macleay)

Springer Spaniel puppies.

If you like what you see, it is normal to pay a deposit, usually about £100, to book your puppy, which will be ready to go at eight weeks old. Make sure that both parents are registered with the British Kennel Club as this goes some way to ensure that the puppy's breeding is what it is supposed to be, and, as you may want to breed from the dog in the future, the puppies can then be registered.

BUYING AN OLDER PUPPY

Another method of acquiring a Spaniel is to buy a puppy between nine and fourteen months old. A good source for such dogs is the field trial fraternity, as most field triallers tend to buy or breed three or four pups at a time and run them on until they decide which dog or dogs they prefer, at which point they will usually sell on the others. Sometimes these dogs have had some training and it is a simple matter to carry on school-

ing the dog in the normal way. There are both advantages and disadvantages to buying an older puppy. The most obvious advantage is that it saves a lot of time in rearing a small puppy and you can see exactly what you are buying instead of waiting for a year until the puppy grows into a young adult. Most of the young dogs sold on by triallers are perfectly sound, and the reason they are for sale is that the owner prefers one of the others. They will normally be of the finest breeding and should be given serious consideration in your quest for a gundog. The main disadvantage to buying an older dog is that you may lack the close bond that is built up between dog and owner through rearing a puppy to adulthood. However, personally I find that after a few weeks playing with the new dog, he soon builds up his confidence and trust in you, and a bond will form, just as with a young puppy. When I buy a young Spaniel, whether partly trained or completely untouched, I find it is always a good idea to go back to the beginning, teaching the dog the basics from the very start of training and slowly progressing through the various stages of schooling the dog, as outlined later in this book.

MINOR BREEDS

There are various less common breeds of Spaniel, including Clumber Spaniels, Welsh Springer Spaniels and Suffolk Spaniels to name a few. These dogs are occasionally seen in the shooting field and are usually owned and handled by breed enthusiasts who quite rightly want to give their animals a chance to perform in the field the tasks they were originally bred to do. Through much patience and perseverance, the owners of these dogs can and do successfully train them to carry out the required skills, although they can never reach the level of competence of the English Springer or Cocker Spaniels. These minor breeds tend to be kept nowadays by show enthusiasts whose interests lie first and foremost in the show ring and in the promotion of their particular breed, rather than in producing a competent gundog with the temperament and abilities that we in the shooting field require. Working English Springers and Cockers are bred almost exclusively by sportsmen for sportsmen, and it stands to reason therefore that to overlook this point because you would prefer a

ABOVE: *Clumber Spaniel. (Photo: Helen Macleay)*

BOTTOM LEFT: *Welsh Springer Spaniel. (Photo: Helen Macleay)*

BOTTOM RIGHT: *Suffolk Spaniel. (Photo: Helen Macleay)*

different breed will hamper your chances of success from the beginning. However, if you are already the proud owner of one of the rarer Spaniel breeds and would like to give your dog some training, the procedure is exactly as outlined in this book. It may take a little longer but good results can be obtained with patience and perseverance.

DOG OR BITCH?

In deciding whether a male or a female is best suited to your situation, a few points must be taken into consideration. Firstly, if there is already a male dog in the household, then bringing a bitch (female) into the family may cause problems as the new puppy will, after its first year, come into season twice a year, and the dogs will have to be kept apart for twenty-one days. During this time the dog may show signs of stress, perhaps going off his food, urinating everywhere and generally behaving abnormally. Around one week before the bitch comes into season she starts producing scent, which nature has designed to attract males so that when she becomes receptive to breeding, between eleven and fifteen days after the first sign of blood, there will be a dog present to mate with. Even when the two are kept apart, the dog will still behave in this way as nature and his brain are telling him he must get to her. Obviously the same problem will arise if you already own a bitch and buy a male puppy.

Likewise, during the time that the female is receptive to breeding, she will do everything in her power to get to a male, including running away and climbing out of kennels and so on. During this period of her season it is not possible to take her to shoots (or anywhere really where other dogs are present). This must be taken into consideration if you choose a female. It is often said that bitches are trouble for three weeks of the shooting season, whereas dogs are trouble all the time. This is not true, of course! Dogs are like people in this respect. Some males are very kind and gentle-natured, whereas some bitches can be hard and excitable in character. This all comes down to the individual animal and is nothing at all to do with the sex of the dog. Personally, when I am choosing a puppy from a litter, I tend to pick the one that I like and the one that shows interest in its surroundings, rather than choosing one because of its sex. Some experienced handlers prefer dogs, and others bitches. It is entirely a matter of personal preference that can only be decided through experience with various dogs.

THE NEW DOG IN THE HOME

Bringing a new puppy home for the first time can be a daunting experience, especially if the puppy whines, barks and will not settle. Meanwhile the new owner is trying to work out if the puppy is hungry, thirsty, needs to go outside or just wants some attention. It is perfectly normal for a puppy to behave in this way; many will try to hide under the furniture or in corners. This does not mean that he has been mistreated in any way or that he has a nervous disposition. Remember that your new pup spent the first eight weeks of his short life in the company of his siblings, playing, fighting and competing for food, with mum regularly there for comfort, cleaning and feeding. With feral dogs a bitch and her litter will stay more or less together until the pups are around five months old; by this time they will be exploring a bit further each day, learning to hunt and acquire food for themselves while still being fed by their mother, who will regurgitate food for them. As time passes, however, her visits become less and less frequent, thus forcing the pups to go their separate ways to hunt for food, eventually becoming completely independent. It is not difficult, therefore, to understand the shock your pup must feel when at just eight weeks old he is removed from a world where he feels secure and confident and is plunged into a strange new place. A few days of simple routine and quality time spent with the new puppy will soon integrate him into the household, and he will then accept you and your family as his new pack.

In practical terms I find it best to use a dog crate placed in the corner of the room; from here, the puppy will be able to see and hear what is going on around him, while feeling secure in his own little space. The crate should be furnished with some bedding, a few toys and, of course, water and food. The first thing he will want to do when he comes out of the crate is clean himself, and it's a simple matter to carry him straight

My son Craig with his new Cocker Spaniel puppy.

outside where he can relieve himself. In this way you are house-training the puppy from the start. A crate is also useful for an older puppy, as they can become quite destructive if left to their own devices. At night, or if you need to leave him for any length of time during the day, it is much better to put your puppy in his crate with a bone or chewy toy, which he will chew for hours.

The puppy should be taken out of the crate as often as possible and allowed to explore his new surroundings and play. Young puppies need to be fed four times a day initially and water should be available at all times. I am not going to comment on feeding, vaccinations and treating parasites in this book as there is already sufficient literature on these subjects, written by people much more qualified to do so than me. It is sufficient for me to say that as soon as possible after buying your puppy, you should make an appointment with a qualified veterinarian to have his health checked; the vet will also give advice on feeding, vaccinations and parasite control.

I find it best to use a dog crate for a new puppy.

CHAPTER 2

PREPARING A PUPPY FOR TRAINING

THE FIRST SIX MONTHS

The first six months of a young pup's life is a very important learning period, as during this time, due to his inquisitive nature and as the result of exploring new things, he learns how to behave. Puppies learn through trial and error: for example, if your puppy is pulling at a piece of wood and somehow it falls and hits him, you can rest assured he won't do that again. This can be turned to your advantage to teach him some important lessons. For example, if he is pulling at an electrical cable, all that is necessary is to make a loud bang with a rolled-up newspaper close to the cable while he is doing it, giving him the required fright. As soon as he lets go of the cable, give him plenty of praise. Action and reaction is how we teach the puppy what is

Spaniels have a very strong retrieving instinct.

Praise him and let him hold on to the object for a while.

acceptable behaviour and what is not. In a pack situation the adults in the pack would teach the puppy in exactly the same way, by encouraging him to hunt and play, but discouraging him from dangerous situations by giving him a nip or a shake.

Unfortunately, during these early stages it is very easy for the novice trainer to make a few catastrophic mistakes, which can affect a Spaniel puppy for the rest of its life and can be difficult to correct. We have bred a strong retrieving instinct into the Spaniel and when he comes across a slipper, shoe or TV remote, his instinct is to pick it up and carry it around – whereupon all too often he is shouted at, chased around the house and the object roughly pulled out of his mouth. Being an intelligent little animal, he quickly learns from this not to retrieve! Instead, you should encourage the puppy to bring the object to you, praising him as he does so, and let him hold the object for a few moments before giving the command 'Leave' and gently taking it from him with more praise. In this way you are developing the dog's retrieving instinct. The only effective way of avoiding the problem is not to leave things lying around for the puppy to carry off. Obviously this is very difficult when there are young children in the household, and it can be frustrating when the kids undo all your careful work

by playing tug-of-war with a teddy bear or chasing the puppy around the garden trying to get Buzz Lightyear back. This may be great fun, but it is the ruination of many a gundog.

If the children are old enough, try to explain what you and the pup will be doing and why they must not throw sticks and toys for him or play tug-of-war games; instead, encourage them to take him for walks on the leash or to the park where they can chase each other around, meet other dogs and people and generally explore the big wide world.

Another common mistake, which happens when the pup has found something more interesting and won't come back when called, is to run after him. This invariably becomes a chase game, which puppies enjoy immensely, therefore encouraging this behaviour. The correct action is to run away from him and hide if necessary, calling his name and encouragement. He will soon realize that his pack leader has disappeared and he will start to look for you. When he finds you, give him plenty of praise and let him go and play again. He won't go as far this time and he will be listening for your call as it is the warning that you will disappear if he doesn't respond. This method works because a dog is first and foremost a pack animal and he wants to be part of the pack; he feels confident when he is in the group, but when left on his own he becomes nervous and vulnerable.

What I am trying to explain to readers is that you must think about what you are doing and the way your actions and reactions appear from the puppy's point of view. For instance, he may run off to play with another dog and when he eventually does come back, you scold him or chastise him for running off. But in the dog's mind, he is being punished for the last thing he did – coming back – not for running off in the first place. Thus he will quickly learn not to come back at all, or to flit around you rather than coming right up to you for praise, which is what we want at this point.

EARLY RETRIEVING

From a very early age the Spaniel's retrieving instinct is evident and it is a simple matter to encourage your puppy's instincts by regular, very short sessions from the start; puppies as young as eight weeks old will chase and retrieve small objects as part of a game. I find a sock rolled into a tight ball is excellent for the purpose. As with all training, there should be no distractions. Let the puppy see the object, wave it about in front of him and then roll it away a short distance, allowing him to run after it and pick it up; when he does so, you should back away, encouraging him towards you giving praise and attention. Don't take the object from him straight away; let him hold it for a time, all the while rubbing his back and head and encouraging him to stay with you. Eventually you can take the object gently from his mouth with plenty of praise.

With pups up to the age of nine months to a year, I never try to steady them (stop them running in). This has got to be a game for the puppy and he must not have any pressure put on him at this young age. Personally I find it best to take the puppy out two or three

Run away from the puppy, calling his name.

RIGHT: *A sock rolled into a tight ball is excellent for teaching puppies to retrieve.*

BELOW: *Teaching puppy retrieving.*

times a week, allowing no more than three retrieves per session, as in this way the puppy never gets bored with the game and becomes more keen as the months go by. As the puppy grows you can replace the sock or whatever you are using with a tennis ball, then with a half-pound puppy canvas dummy and finally with a one-pound standard dummy. Gradually lengthen the retrieves from just a metre or so with a smaller puppy to as far as you can throw the canvas dummy with the older puppy. During this latter stage, I start throwing the dummy into some light cover or long grass, which encourages him to hunt and use his nose along with his sight.

One important point I would like to make at this stage is never to start any serious training, as outlined later in the book, while the puppy is too young. Many gundogs are ruined by novice trainers starting training too early. You will know when the dog is ready for training, when he becomes boisterous and bold and starts hunting for himself. Up until at least nine months old he is just a baby and he should be allowed to mature naturally; this allows him to develop his natural hunting ability and trainability, which we can then mould into the desired product. The early months are far better spent introducing him to new situations, meeting people, cars, water, children and other dogs, and so on.

On no account be tempted to take your youngster to a shoot 'to let him see what it's all about' or 'to see what a pheasant is'. Spaniels in particular should be kept away from game and shooting until they are almost fully trained and have been taught the necessary skills and commands in the correct order. Once they have realized how much fun game and shooting can be, it is very difficult then to teach them the proper way to behave.

Training must be done in sequence to be successful. You would not expect a child to go to university before having spent seven years at primary school, and another six years or so at secondary school. Yet it never ceases to amaze me how many people take a young dog to a shoot with little or no training and expect him to behave; then, when the time comes to train the dog, he already has in his mind the bad habits that he has learned and any kind of proper training then becomes difficult or impossible.

EARLY LEAD TRAINING

Note: the check chain and extending leash (as described later in this book) should never be used on younger animals.

I use a small leather collar and leather leash. The collar should first be put on the puppy and left for a few days until he becomes accustomed to it. At first he might scratch at it and shake his head; this is quite normal and he will stop after an hour or so. The next step is to clip the leash onto the collar and to allow him to walk around for a while trailing the leash behind him. I leave it on for around half an hour before removing it, repeating the process on subsequent days. Never leave the dog unsupervised while he is trailing the leash, as obviously it could become trapped and, as the dog is unaccustomed to being restrained in this way, he may panic and choke himself. When the puppy becomes accustomed to the leash following him around, pick up the end and call him to you, giving the leash a gentle tug. The puppy might struggle a bit, but with gentle and firm encouragement he will soon stop his nonsense and accept he is on the leash and can't run around as before. Don't attempt to train him to walk to heel at this stage; if he's pulling too hard, stop and jerk him back, giving the 'Heel' command, and then walk on. Remember that he is still very young and needs plenty of free time and exercise in order to mature properly and attain his potential.

INTRODUCTION TO LIVESTOCK

Introducing your pup to livestock is best done at around six months old. Make sure you have the permission of the landowner or farmer, as they will not take kindly to a stranger and his dog chasing their sheep, cattle or horses around a field uninvited.

I am very lucky in this respect as I have access to semi-tame goats on the farm next door. The goats are used to mother orphaned lambs and they are kept in a small field in front of the farmhouse, which saves a lot of leg-work trying to get close enough to a flock of fast, wild sheep. Livestock chasing is much easier dealt with when the dog is young, and before any problem

Children are fantastic for socializing puppies.

has arisen. Once a dog starts chasing sheep, it is very difficult to stop him and it quickly becomes a habit. It is all down to the dog's hunting instinct. I have found repeatedly that if a tame sheep just stands there, then the dog will show little or no interest, and a few will go over and have a sniff. It is the fact that most sheep run away that makes the dog's hunting instinct kick in, and off he goes in pursuit. I am talking through experience when I say that the best Olympic athletes in the world could never even get close to catching a dog in full flight after sheep.

At this point I would like to disprove a few popular 'cures' for chasing. These include:

1. Putting the offender in with a ram in a small pen, whereupon the ram will butt the dog and face him up, which they invariably do. I have tried this method on various occasions with clients' 'sheep chasers', with absolutely no success due to the fact that it is the sheep running away that encourages the dog to chase, while a sheep standing facing the dog offers no temptation at all.

2. Placing the dog in a pen with a ewe and her lamb. This is another method that doesn't work for exactly the same reason as above. The ewe will get between the lamb and the dog and face him up, and there is no fun in that for the dog. However, put the same ewe and lamb in an open field five minutes later and they will run away – and the offender will be off like a rocket in pursuit.

It is much better to address the problem before it arises. It is a simple matter of taking your pup into a small field with some livestock and walking him around on the leash; when he shows any interest at all in the animals, jerk on the leash with the firm command 'No!',

Allow the puppy to trail the leash for half an hour or so every day while you are present.

Introducing a young Spaniel to livestock.

spoken harshly. This is usually all that is necessary. Of course, the process must be repeated regularly to be effective and should be carried out with cattle, horses and chickens wherever and whenever the opportunity arises. Later in the puppy's training, when he has started on the check chain and flexi-lead, a retrieve in a sheep field is also a useful exercise; as you are still in complete control of the dog, any tendency on his part to run towards the sheep can be reprimanded instantly. He will learn very quickly that livestock are not for chasing. He will start to ignore them and treat them as just another part of the landscape.

However, if your dog is a persistent sheep chaser, send him to a reputable dog trainer for a few weeks to have him stop the habit completely. A contract and guarantee should be given and no money should change hands until a demonstration is performed.

INTRODUCTION TO WATER

Spaniels are not generally natural water dogs in the sense that Labradors are. Spaniels need to be taught to enter the water and I find five to six months old is the ideal age to start. It is best to begin during the summer months when the water is warmer and more pleasant for him to play in. Encourage him to get his feet wet by playing with him next to a shallow stream, ideally with gently sloping banks, and with water no more than ten to twelve inches deep. The puppy can splash about without suddenly getting out of his depth, which can cause him to panic.

By this stage your pup should already be chasing and retrieving a tennis ball. I throw a short retrieve alongside the water and let him run in and pick it just to get him in the mood. I then throw the next one to

Giving the pupil a retrieve next to sheep.

Introducing a puppy to water.

Throw the ball just in the water.

An older dog can help encourage a puppy to enter water.

the water's edge, just enough for him to wet his feet as he fetches the ball and brings it back to you. He might be slightly worried at first but if you encourage him he will soon be splashing around at the edge. By slowly increasing the distance that you throw the ball, and introducing slightly deeper water, your puppy should soon be swimming around happily after two or three visits to the stream.

Another good method is to use an older dog to persuade the puppy to enter water. Allow the puppy to run around as you give the older dog a few retrieves into the water, and he will soon want to join in the fun and try to beat his old friend to the ball. Once the puppy is entering the water confidently, do exactly the same thing in deeper water encouraging him to swim;

again a gradual banking is much easier for the pup than a plunge into the deep. Never throw the pup into the water as this will only serve to put him off and will make your job much more difficult. It must be a game for the pup and he has to enjoy it. That is all you are looking for at this stage and a trip to the water once every week or so keeps him keen, serving to make things very easy when it comes to teaching more advanced water work, as described later in the book.

EARLY HUNTING

The Spaniel is first and foremost a hunter, and you must encourage your young dog to hunt at every opportunity. Although the hunting instinct is normally very

Young Spaniel hunting naturally.

strong and little effort is required on the part of the trainer, this is not always the case and some young Spaniels need to be taught. It is also very important at this stage not to inhibit the dog's hunting ability. This often happens if the trainer attempts to train and control the dog while he is still too young and immature; remember that a puppy must develop naturally to achieve his full potential. He will learn to hunt the wind and quarter the ground freely, although at this stage he does not (and should not) know what he is hunting. He will find all the scent he is picking up really interesting and exciting, as we have bred this love of game scent into our dogs through years of selective breeding.

One of the best ways to do this is to take the pup occasionally to a field where there is short-ish grass and where rabbits have been feeding overnight, but there must be no rabbits visible. Release the pup and let him sniff around; he will start showing interest immediately. I encourage this with a snap of my fingers, along with the verbal command 'Get on' and I repeat these commands all the time the pup is exploring the new scents. In this way, by gentle repetition once or twice a week, I am teaching him the hunt command without him even realizing he is being taught, and I am in no way putting any pressure on him or inhibiting his instinctive curiosity and ability.

There is absolutely no need to take your puppy to a rabbit pen (a fenced-off area containing semi-tame rabbits). In fact, the last thing you want is to have him chasing rabbits around; you should be encouraging him to use his nose and not his sight. Once he gets the idea, take him to some very light cover and repeat the process. By gradually increasing the length and density of cover, he will come to love being deep in the undergrowth exploring and rooting around. It is inevitable that eventually he will come across a rabbit or pheasant, flush it and give chase. When you eventually catch him, do not chastise him or give him a scolding; what he has done is perfectly natural, and as long as it doesn't happen too often there will be no harm done.

TIME TO START TRAINING

Proper training can start when your puppy is around ten months to a year old. You will know when the time is right as he will start getting too confident, disappearing out of sight and generally becoming troublesome when taken out for his exercise. Now is the time to take things in hand and start basic training. It is best, I find, to start your training when you will have twenty to thirty minutes free time every day for two or three months. This is obviously more simple in the summer months with lighter evenings and longer days, especially when teaching puppies the basics, as they seem to benefit from short training sessions given daily.

Starting training later in the dog's life is not a problem. I have trained as gundogs Spaniels that had had no training whatsoever until I took them on at around two years old. However, they had been family pets, were well socialized and had never been introduced to game. I actually found them very easy to train as they had grown out of all the puppy nonsense, but were still very keen to learn and enjoyed it immensely.

To reiterate, start training your puppy somewhere between the ages of ten and sixteen months old; the best time is probably somewhere in the middle. There seems to be a period at around this age when the young dog's brain acts like a sponge soaking up all the information and training we give him, making our job very simple.

CHAPTER 3

TEACHING THE BASICS

So, you've decided it's time to start some serious training with your adolescent dog, who is bursting with energy and all the natural ability we've bred into the Spaniel for many years.

Training is a simple matter of moulding the abilities we require into the obedient animal, without inhibiting his natural hunting or retrieving skills. Training gundogs (or any dog for that matter) can be likened to building a house. If the foundations are weak or poorly built, cracks will appear and the house will fall down before completion. It is the same with dog training. Unless the basics of sit, stay, heel and recall are 100 per cent reliable, the training process will be unable to progress and will ultimately fail.

Most novice trainers are so keen to get on with the more interesting advanced training that they skip over the basics. They want their dog doing 100-metre retrieves and hunting up game before it even stops to the whistle and walks to heel. This is the biggest and most common mistake people can make while training a dog. The importance of teaching basics to a high standard cannot be stressed enough. What use is a hard-hunting Spaniel if it is flushing game 100 metres in front of its handler, chasing the bird into the next field and flushing more game? I've seen it many times. And it's not the dog's fault – it is down to the trainer's failure to teach the dog the most basic command: to stop to the whistle.

The correct position for the check chain.

The flexi lead and check chain.

Once a Spaniel gets keen on hunting up and chasing game, its instincts are so strong that it is very difficult or impossible to stop. Thus the dog should be almost fully trained before it is put in a position where it can flush a bird or rabbit. I am always amazed at the number of people I see at shoots with five- and six-month-old dogs running around chasing everything and anything. They are 'just giving the dog some experience', or 'letting it hear some shots'. In fact, what they are doing is ruining a perfectly good prospect.

GETTING STARTED

The first item you need is a check chain attached to an extending leash. The check chain should fit the dog with about six inches of slack around his neck, and must be put on correctly, with the ring that slides coming up from the bottom of the dog's neck (with the dog on the left-hand side). I recommend a 5-metre heavy flexi lead, with cord rather than tape. This piece of equipment is invaluable in dog training, although it takes some time and practice to master. It allows

the trainer to be in complete control throughout basic training, avoiding frustration, as the dog cannot go wrong.

WALKING TO HEEL

The secret of teaching a dog to walk to heel is that you refuse to walk on if the dog's head is in front of your leg. If he goes forward, stop dead and snap the check chain back. As soon as the dog is in the correct position, proceed to walk on. In this way you are teaching the dog to follow your leg. The check chain should be slack at all times. The click sound made when the chain is snapped back has the desired effect, along with the command 'Heel'.

There is one important point, however. You are telling the dog to heel, not asking him. As with all commands, do not shout, but give it sharply and clearly. Remember that if you do not give a clear command, the dog cannot possibly understand what is required. When I am training dogs to heel, I walk in zigzags, and make lots of ninety degree turns, snapping the lead towards

Heel work is very important for any gundog.

me as I turn. I also vary the speed at which I walk, trying to 'trick' the dog into going in front, whereupon I stop, snap the lead back and give the 'Heel' command.

Some Spaniel trainers do not teach their dogs to walk to heel as they believe it inhibits the dog's hunting. I do not agree with this simply because I don't want to have a dog on a leash when I'm shooting or 'on pick up', as there is always the risk of the leash getting tangled in your legs or branches, and it is completely impractical. A dog taught properly to walk to heel has an invisible lead (your control), which does not affect hunting ability in any way.

INTRODUCING THE STOP COMMAND

The best place to teach these basic commands is on a short, flat, grassy field with few or no distractions; these will be introduced later. While I am teaching 'Heel' and introducing the 'Stop, sit', I blow the whistle along with the appropriate hand signal. I use ACME 210½ whistles as opposed to the stag horn or buffalo horn as they are replaceable and always sound exactly the same. The stop whistle is one short, sharp 'Toot', given in conjunction with a snap of the check chain and the hand signal. The moment the dog sits, praise it with a pat on the head and say 'Good dog'. This lets the dog know he has performed the action well.

My first training session lasts about five minutes. In this way we are not worrying or pressurizing the dog in any way, and he will be keen to go training again tomorrow. As the training progresses, the sessions become gradually longer and longer, and you can introduce

Introducing the 'Stop, Sit' whistle, along with the correct hand signal.

the dog to new commands whilst always going over the lessons previously taught. It is a case of one step forwards, two steps back throughout the dog's training. We are simply adding exercise after exercise to our training sessions, whilst all the time reinforcing the exercises already taught. In this way we are engraining the commands into the dog's mind, until it becomes habit for the dog to obey. Dogs pick up habits very quickly, good and bad, and we can use this to our advantage.

By repeating the same commands over and over and enforcing the required action by use of the check chain, you are building a habit that then becomes an automatic response, no matter what the dog is doing – and that is exactly what we need in a gundog. When he

hears the whistle, he stops. This can only be achieved by repetition. I find it best to train the dog every day for a short period. This is the best way for the dog to learn quickly, and prevents the dog getting bored and losing interest. It is also a distinct advantage if the dog is now kennelled when not being trained. Not only does this give him his own space, but he will look forward to his training sessions and respects you more when you take him out. It also reduces the possibility of wives/ husbands and children throwing sticks for him or playing tug of war, and generally undoing your good work.

'SIT, STAY'

When the dog has learned to walk to heel and sit to

Dogs are more receptive to training when kennelled.

Giving the verbal command 'Stay'.

the whistle command whilst at heel on the check chain and extending lead, you can introduce the 'Sit, stay' command. This command is very important as it is the basis of teaching the dog steadiness, as well as enabling the recall and the use of hand signals. After spending a few minutes doing heel work and sit commands, use the stop whistle to sit the dog beside you, then turn and face him. As you do this, hold your hand up and give the command 'Stay' as you back away a few paces. If he tries to follow you, flick the check chain and go towards him, again using the verbal 'Stay' command. When he gets the idea, walk back to him and praise him with a pat on the head and say 'Good dog'. Gradually extend the distance until you reach the limit of your extending lead.

INTRODUCING THE RECALL

The standard recall command is two short sharp toots on the whistle and you stand with your arms spread. It is important at this point to note that the use of treats and food in training a working Spaniel is a big NO for two reasons. Firstly, we want the dog to obey our command because we told him, not because he's hungry or wants a treat. Secondly, when the dog is starting to retrieve, he will approach you, drop the dummy and expect to be given a treat, instead of delivering the dummy to hand. So never use treats as a shortcut to training your dog.

Over the years I have probably tried every method of training dogs. The system I have outlined in this book always works. As a professional trainer, I cannot afford to fail. Therefore there is nothing written in this book that is not pertinent to the final result. For training to succeed, the dog must accept that you are the pack leader; he must trust and rely on you for food, exercise and guidance. I tell my pupils to be aloof from their dogs for the duration of training. Stop petting the dog and fussing over him. He is a dog, and he has dog needs, not human needs. And what he needs most is a dominant leader, whereupon he can relax and let the boss make decisions. You cannot train a dog unless he respects you as pack leader.

Giving the 'Recall' command.

My method works because dogs crave positive attention from their leader. It stands to reason therefore that if you are constantly petting and fussing the dog all the time, then when you want to praise him for a correct action, it means nothing to the dog as he gets this level of attention day and night. In short, withhold affection during training, and limit its use to praising the dog for carrying out the desired action. In this way the dog is learning to obey commands without any punishment or chastisement having to be given. Remember, too, that if the dog gets it wrong then it is not his fault but the trainer's, who has perhaps taken a step too far too soon. Next day start again and slow things down, taking smaller steps.

The easy way to teach your Spaniel the recall is to use the stop whistle to sit the dog at your side, as you have been doing for the last week or so. Face him, tell him to 'Stay' and back away. When the extending leash is fully extended, give two short sharp toots on the whistle and a tug on the leash, and he will be on his way towards you. Encourage him with plenty of praise and repeat the process.

You are now in a position to alternate between recalling him to you or you returning to the dog. As I said previously, dogs pick up habits and routines very quickly. If you carry out the various training exercises in the same order every day, then within days the dog will have learnt the routine. It is important to vary the order of exercises, as this allows the Spaniel to learn the commands and not just the routine, which at this stage is vital as you do not want your dog to anticipate what you are going to ask him to do. He must wait for the command.

THE RETRIEVE

Once the dog has become proficient at all the exercises listed here, it is time to introduce the basic marked

The dog is easily controlled by a tug on the check chain.

retrieve. This is done with the dog still on his check chain and extending leash. As outlined in the previous chapter, 'Preparing your Puppy for Training', your dog has been allowed to run and pick up a tennis ball or small dummy. You are now going to teach the dog steadiness: that is, not going to retrieve the dummy until commanded to do so. Still in a flat, short grass field, sit the dog at your side using the stop whistle and snap of chain, engage the lock on the extending leash and throw the dummy a few metres or so away. The dog will try to run in and pick the dummy. However, you've got him on the chain. Make him sit by snapping the chain in conjunction with the stop whistle. When he has settled, point to the dummy and encourage him with the command 'Go back'. You must remember to release the lock on the extending leash before sending him, and never throw the dummy further than the extending leash allows (about 5 metres). He should pick the dummy, but he can't do anything but bring it to you as you are in control of the leash. If there is a problem, encourage him to you by use of the recall whistle and, if necessary, by a tug of the leash. Do not be in a rush at this point to take the dummy from the dog. Let him hold it; in fact, you should encourage him to hold it by not touching the dummy. Make a fuss of him, rub his head and back and give him plenty of praise. When you

Teaching the Spaniel to be steady to the thrown dummy.

Teaching the 'Go back' command.

Gently hold the dummy and give the 'Leave' command.

think the time is right, gently take hold of the dummy and give the command 'Leave'. Never jerk the dummy from the dog's mouth, as rough behaviour like this can cause problems later with the delivery of the dummy to hand. If the dog's delivery is not perfect at this point, ignore it and carry on with training, as this is much easier dealt with later in the dog's training process. I deal with this subject later in the book.

SITTING TO THE WHISTLE AT A DISTANCE

At this point in training I start to encourage the dog to stop a short distance from the handler. Initially, I find the easiest way is to give the 'Sit, stay' command, walk

away to the full length of the leash and give the 'Recall' command; then, when the dog is about halfway back to you, raise your arm to the 'Stop' signal while simultaneously blowing the stop whistle and taking a step or two towards the dog. As soon as he sits, go to him and praise him. Do not repeat this exercise during a lesson. Once is enough, because he will begin to anticipate you stopping him, and this will slow down his recall. So, in short, for every time you stop the dog on his return to you, call him right to you five times. In this way you are maintaining a fast recall and teaching the dog to stop to the whistle. Take every opportunity you can at this point to stop the dog when he is messing about at scent or when he is distracted. Blow the stop whistle, raise your hand and take a few steps towards

Teaching the stop whistle.

him. As soon as he sits, say 'Good boy', and give plenty of praise.

It stands to reason that if your dog doesn't sit to the command instantly when he is beside you, he will not sit at 5 metres away and will certainly not stop at 30 metres. So the stop whistle should be taught gradually, starting beside you, then at a few metres away, gradually increasing the distance until you have reached the limit of the extending leash. That's far enough for now.

TEACHING THE SEND-BACK

Your daily training sessions should last about ten to fifteen minutes at this point. Always start with 'Sit', 'Stay', 'Heel' and 'Recall', adding to these basics whenever possible. The next exercise I teach is the send-back. This is a very useful exercise. You are teaching your Spaniel to walk to heel/sit to whistle/steadiness to thrown dummy, and also building up his memory, all in one exercise.

I teach this with the dog still on a check chain and extending leash. Sit the dog beside you as previously, then walk forward with the dog at heel for a few paces. From this point throw the dummy a few metres or so ahead, but instead of sending him for the retrieve, turn away and walk him a few paces back towards where you started. Then turn around, point to the dummy and give the verbal 'Go back' command; take delivery as normal with plenty of praise. It is important to note that you must never send the dog further than the leash allows, as the resulting jerk to a sudden stop may frighten the dog, and then he won't leave your side for a few days.

LOSING THE CHECK CHAIN AND EXTENDING LEASH

So far all the training has been done with the dog on a chain and extending leash, and he should never have been allowed off the leash. You will have been training

A short send-back using the extending leash and check chain.

Alternate between having the dog on and off the extending leash and chain.

him for between three and four weeks, which is plenty of time for him to have built up the habit of obeying all the commands taught so far. It is now time to gradually reduce the time he spends on the leash and extend the time that he is loose.

To do this correctly is very simple. You do not want the dog to think 'freedom, I can do what I like'. When I think the time is right, halfway through a training session when the dog is walking beside me at heel, I work my hand down the leash and gently unclip it from the chain and carry on with the daily training regime. I only do this for a few minutes though, before putting

him back on the chain. The next day I do the same thing, and gradually build up the time the dog is off the leash. This process should take about a week to complete and eventually you can discard the check chain also.

You are now in a position to give your pupil longer send-backs and to stop giving marked retrieves almost completely, as these now teach the dog nothing new. When you can send your dog back from your side for a 50 metre send-back, that is enough for a young Spaniel. You are now halfway to having the trained Spaniel you wished for.

CHAPTER 4

TEACHING HUNTING

Hunting and flushing game for the sportsman to shoot is the primary role of the Spaniel. It is therefore very important that you train the dog to hunt correctly and within shooting range. There is nothing worse than a Spaniel consistently flushing game too far out; this is very frustrating and ruins the day's shooting for everyone concerned.

Most well bred Spaniels will hunt naturally; in fact, I have never come across one who did not hunt to some degree. The skill of the trainer is to teach the dog to hunt for the handler and not for itself, which the majority of Spaniels seen at shoots are doing, paying no heed to anything or anybody. Once a Spaniel's nose is engaged, his brain and hearing are in neutral, and

Rushes that are too dense or long will snag the flexi lead. This field is perfect.

Spaniel hunting a head wind correctly.

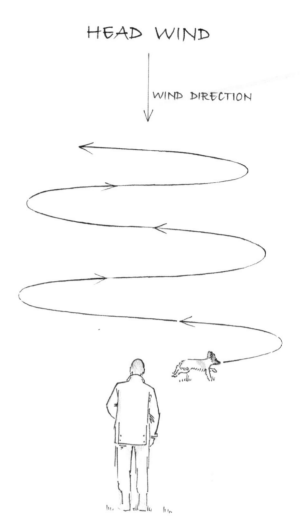

HEAD WIND

WIND DIRECTION

when he gets to this stage it is nearly impossible to correct him. You must teach the Spaniel to hunt within range and to obey whistle and verbal commands from the start. It is very tempting to take your young dog shooting when he is only half-trained and he may seem to be doing well for a few outings, but once he picks up on what he's doing, stopping him or keeping him in range will be impossible.

When training Spaniels, or any of the hunting retrieving breeds, I always keep the hunting and the retrieving aspects totally separate for as long as possible, and until both disciplines have been thoroughly learned. On alternate days I teach retrieving, the other days I teach hunting. In this way I keep it simple for the dog, and it also benefits him in remaining steady to flush and eventually to shot.

GETTING STARTED

I like to teach hunting in light cover or in rushes that are not too long or dense as they will snag the flexi lead. It is always an advantage if there is a little game scent, although it is not necessary at this stage as the Spaniel will hunt anyway. Another very important point to take into consideration when teaching your dog hunting is the direction of the wind. Always start early hunting training by walking slowly into the wind as he will naturally quarter across wind.

I use the flexi lead and check chain as outlined in previous chapters. Sit the dog in front of you with the whistle command and hand signal. Then cast the dog off with a snap of the fingers while moving your arm in the required direction as you slowly walk into the wind.

The dog should take off hunting in that direction. When he reaches around 3 or 4 metres from the handler, two toots on the whistle (the recall) and a tug on the flexi lead will turn him back towards you, whereupon you should turn and walk across wind in the opposite direction from him. He will always want to be in front of you so will naturally cross in that direction; as he does so, snap your fingers and move your arm in that direction, therefore encouraging him to cross the wind as far as the flexi lead allows, which is 3 or 4 metres. Then repeat the two toots on the whistle and encourage him in the opposite direction again.

At this point it is worth mentioning that 3 or 4 metres may not seem very far out for the dog to be hunting,

Casting the dog off with a snap of the fingers to hunt into the required direction.

Two toots on the stop whistle and a tug on the leash will turn him back towards you.

but I keep him close for two reasons: firstly, as the dog gains experience he will naturally pull out and cover more ground; and secondly, if you can't control the dog well when he is close to you, it will be impossible when he is further out.

This exercise should be repeated for five or six minutes' duration every alternate day for around two weeks until he has got into the habit of obeying the turn (recall) signal.

THE STOP COMMAND

It is now time to introduce the 'Stop' command', which is one toot on the whistle and a hand held up. I find the best way to do this is to give the command as the dog is crossing close to you, along with a snap of the flexi lead and chain and, if necessary, a quick step or two towards the dog with your hand up in the stop position. As soon as he stops and sits, give him plenty of praise and cast him off hunting again. The stop command should only be given two or three times during the five minute hunting lesson, as any more than this can cause him to anticipate you stopping him and subsequently slow down his hunting. Remember the skill of dog training is teaching the dog to obey commands without inhibiting his natural ability. On this occasion, 'a little not too often' is the way to proceed.

After a few days, when he is obeying the command quickly and reliably as he passes you on his 'beat', stop him slightly further from you each day until he will stop instantly at the full distance he is allowed to travel by the flexi lead.

Giving the 'Stop' command.

Useful Advice

- When teaching your Spaniel hunting commands, do not use the same ground every day; try to vary the terrain, i.e. long grass/in bracken/woods and so on. This not only serves to keep him interested, but also gives him experience of different types of terrain and cover.
- Never run a young dog until he is tired. Keep the session short and finish with the dog still keen to do more.
- In hot weather train early in the morning or in the evening when it is cooler, or better still teach water work.
- In the early stages of hunting, it is best to avoid the chance of him contacting game if possible, as a chase at this point can undo all your good work.
- There is absolutely no need to use a starting pistol or similar during the early stages of training. Introduction to shot comes later.
- The stop whistle is the single most important command you will teach the Spaniel, and you must ensure that he stops quickly every single time. Without this control, it is impossible to teach any advanced retrieving/hunting or even flushing live game. This can only be achieved through repetition and consistency on the part of the handler, demanding complete obedience to the whistle command. 'He stops most of the time' is absolutely not acceptable, and the trainer must go back to the basics. Dog training tends to consist of two steps forwards and one step backwards, so it is vital to always return and practise the basics: **'Sit'/'Stay'/ 'Recall'** and, most importantly, **'Stop'**.

DISCARDING THE FLEXI LEAD AND CHAIN

When your pupil is turning reliably to the recall command and sitting to the stop command, it is time to discard the flexi lead. It is very important to do this without the dog realizing that there has been any change to his hunting routine, as the last thing you want is for him to take off into cover when he notices that he is free.

The correct method is to give him a short hunting lesson on the lead. Stop him as usual and when you go forward to praise him for stopping, simply unclip the lead from the check chain and cast him off to hunt again as normal, allowing him to hunt with the chain still around his neck. If done correctly, he will not even notice that he is no longer attached physically to the trainer, and he will continue to obey the commands he has been taught. Carry on the lesson for a few minutes, then stop him, giving praise for the correct action, and clip him back on the lead. That's enough for the day.

After a few days' training with the chain around his neck, you can discard the check chain completely if you are confident that he will obey whistle commands. When you take him from the kennel for his training session, use a normal rope lead or, if you have followed my training method correctly, he will walk to heel until commanded to hunt.

HUNTING A CHEEK (SIDE) WIND

All your training as regards hunting at this stage should have been done with the dog hunting across the head-wind and the trainer zigzagging into the wind. Once the dog is doing this reliably and naturally, it is time to introduce the 'Cheek' wind. With the wind coming from left to right or vice versa, it is impossible for a dog to scent game in front of the handler unless he is in the correct position to do so. The dog should always be cast off downwind as the handler walks slowly at right angles to the wind, and the dog will try to quarter across the wind. You must encourage the dog to hunt at around forty-five degrees to the wind, which allows him to scent any game on your beat. As the dog gains experience, he will learn to hunt the

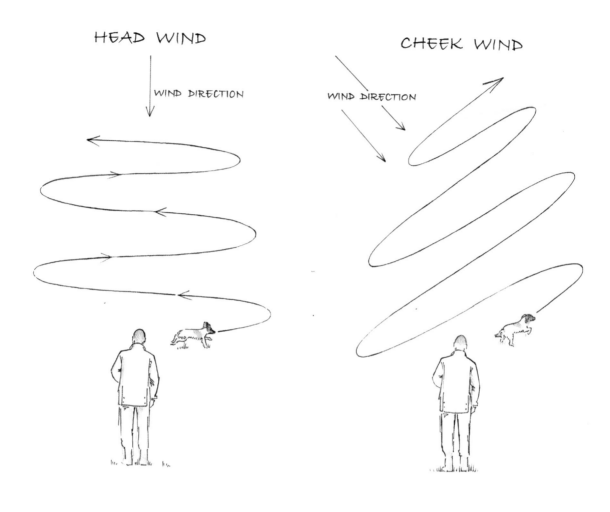

The correct pattern for hunting in a head wind.

The correct pattern for hunting in a cheek wind.

wind properly, ensuring he has the best chance of contacting game without missing any on the ground he will cover.

HUNTING A TAIL WIND

I will outline in this chapter the correct method of hunting a tail wind from behind the dog and handler, although I find it much better to teach the dog this discipline later in the training schedule when the dog has gained some game-finding experience. In some ways it goes against the fact that you are trying to teach

your dog to hunt a tight pattern and not to bore in front, which it has to do to be in a position to scent any game when the wind is behind him.

Your dog, when cast off with a tail wind, will do one of two things. He will either hunt in large 'circles', turning back to take the wind, or he will run straight out and hunt back towards you. Both are correct and as long as you move forward slowly, giving the dog time to cover the ground in front, he will not miss any game. However, if he just hunts normally as in a head wind, then it will be impossible for him to scent the game and he will miss it.

TAIL WIND

WIND DIRECTION

The correct pattern for hunting in a tail wind.

AN OCCASIONAL RETRIEVE

I commented earlier in the chapter on the advantages of keeping hunting and retrieving completely separate. However, there is one exception to this rule: the occasional retrieve. It should never be repeated during a single hunting/training session, and should not be brought into every session – once every two or three outings is quite adequate – as if it is overdone, the dog will stop hunting properly and instead will start running around looking at you and waiting for the thrown dummy.

While the dog is hunting his pattern, blow the stop whistle to stop the dog as he passes you; the instant he sits, throw the dummy while holding your hand in the 'sit/stay' position. Alternate between sending him

for a retrieve and picking the dummy yourself. In this way you will avoid the problem of him anticipating your command, which helps to reinforce steadiness. Once the dog gets the idea, stop him a little further out from you, until he will stop and watch from the furthest point of his beat. I must stress again that you must not carry out this exercise regularly; it is meant to sharpen the dog's reaction to the stop whistle, but he must never anticipate being stopped.

JUMPING FENCES AND GATES

It is at around this stage in the young dog's training that I start teaching him to jump obstacles such as fences and walls, and into cars. This can be an emotive subject, as some handlers insist on not asking their

Author's Comment

I train all types of gundogs, and I noticed that Spaniels, on the whole, were a lot 'sharper' on the whistle, stopping instantly and watching me, whereas Retrievers tended to put on the brakes more slowly with an expression of 'What is he wanting now?' I started incorporating in my Retriever training a similar exercise to the one outlined above, and the result was amazing. The dogs wanted to stop and instantly focused on me. I put this down to the fact that the stop whistle now meant something good (a retrieve was about to happen), and they were not just obliged to sit and wait for a command. Again I discovered that if it is over-done, the exercise had a similar detrimental effect on the Retriever as it did on the Spaniel.

Stopping the dog while hunting and throwing the dummy.

Sending him for the retrieve.

Alternating between picking the dummy yourself and sending the dog helps to establish steadiness.

Teaching the puppy to jump obstacles such as fences.

Encourage the young Spaniel to jump in and out of your vehicle.

dogs to jump fences due to the danger of catching themselves on barbed wire. I do not agree with this view. I firmly believe that a dog, once he has learned to jump confidently and properly, is never or very rarely injured. Most injuries occur when a dog who has not been trained and practised in crossing fences attempts to jump outwith the handler's control. He invariably lands on the top (barbed) wire and an expensive visit to the vet ensues.

Another reason for teaching my dogs to jump on command is that if I am picking up or shooting, I may have a gamebag full of pheasants and/or a gun, as well as four or five dogs, and the last thing I want to be doing is lifting them all over every fence or padlocked gate we encounter. A pleasant day's shooting would

turn into an obstacle course on a par with anything the sergeant-majors in our armed forces could conjure up.

I use the same command for prompting dogs to jump, whether it is into a vehicle or crossing a fence or stream: 'Get over'. It makes absolutely no difference what command is used, but as with all commands, consistency is important. An easy way to teach the dog the command is at feeding time. Take him from his kennel and let him see the bowl of food, then take him to the back of a vehicle and tell him to sit and stay while you open the back door. Place the bowl of food in the car, then, after waiting a few seconds, give the command 'Get over', encouraging him with a snap of the fingers if necessary.

Initially in some cases it may be necessary to lift

A suitable fence.

Encouraging the young Spaniel to jump the fence.

his front feet on to the rear of the car and help him scramble in for his food. Repeat this for a few days if necessary until he jumps in confidently on command. A word of advice here – never lift a young dog into the car or van, unless you wish to do it for the next eleven or twelve years or more, as they very quickly learn that they don't need to jump – they will be lifted in anyway.

The next step is to find a low rabbit net fence with a single strand of plain wire holding it up. These can normally be found surrounding small conifer planta-

A confident jumper.

tions, or you may have to make one. In my area they are very common and I make use of them whenever the opportunity arises.

Having given your dog the 'Sit, stay' command a few metres away from the fence, cross over it a short distance away from him. Give the recall command and, as he approaches the fence, tell him to 'Get over'. If successful, give plenty of praise and repeat the exercise. It may be that you have to lift his front feet onto the top wire and help him over, but with practice he will get the idea.

As he becomes more practised and confident, an occasional retrieve over a low fence will result in him becoming keen on jumping. As his training progresses, send-backs with the 'Get over' command should be given; extending the distance from the fence and the height of the fence will result in a capable and confident jumper.

CHAPTER 5

TEACHING RETRIEVING AND HANDLING

Why teach the Spaniel to handle to a retrieve? In many shooting situations it is very difficult for the handler to get close enough to the fallen game for the dog to retrieve it. For example, a pheasant might have come down on the other side of a river or lake, or on the far side of a fence or hedge, or a duck might be floating in the middle of a lake. Unless the handler enjoys swimming or crawling through prickly hawthorn hedges, it is a distinct advantage to be able to handle the dog out to 100 metres or further to collect the game. It may be that the dog has not seen the pheasant fall (a marked retrieve) as you were at the other side of a wood or hedge. This is where handling to a blind retrieve (unseen to the dog) comes into its own.

It is not difficult to teach the Spaniel to handle, and they pick it up very quickly. The exercises outlined in this chapter should be repeated two or three times a week, gradually extending distances, crossing various obstacles and using different types of cover. In this way you are building up the young dog's confidence in you as a handler, especially when, for example, you give a 'Go back' command, or a 'Left' or 'Right' command, and he finds the dummy easily and retrieves it. Handling is a partnership between the dog and the handler, therefore clear hand and verbal commands must be given in order for the animal to understand what you require of him. When he obeys the command and finds the retrieve (his reward), he has learned the lesson.

I start teaching my Spaniels to handle at around fourteen months old. As outlined previously, I keep the hunting side of things totally separate from the retrieving element until much later in the dog's training. The kingpin of teaching handling is the stop whistle; unless the dog will stop, sit and look at you, it is obviously impossible to give him a directional command. If your dog is not doing this, go back to the basics – a few weeks of you insisting he stops when told should solve the problem.

At this stage I stop giving the dog 'marked retrieves', as this is teaching him nothing new and only serves to wind him up and excite him. This I do not want as it can sometimes lead to the dog squeaking or yipping in excitement, which is a major fault in a gundog and once started is very difficult to stop.

All handling exercises must be in a flat grass field initially, as the dog will see the dummy he is required to pick and go straight to it. At this stage we do not want him to have to hunt for it. When I give him a 'Right' command for instance, I want him to run in a near-straight line for at least 30 or 40 metres in the required direction. A fence line is also a useful tool, especially one that runs straight down the side of my chosen field as it serves to help keep the dog in a straight line. I also use a grass track on occasion as again it keeps the dog focused and moving in the correct direction.

SEND BACK

Walk the dog at heel along the edge of a field, and make him sit beside you using your whistle and hand signal. Make sure he is facing the direction in which you will throw the dummy, which will be parallel to the fence and roughly a metre out from it.

Turn the dog at heel away from the dummy and walk

Throw the dummy parallel to the fence.

back along the fence line for about 50 metres. Turn around, sit the dog beside you, wait a few seconds or so, and then point directly to the dummy and give the command 'Go back', whereupon the dog should run out, pick the dummy and return to you with the retrieve. Give plenty of praise and repeat the exercise, adding a few metres distance every time you do it over the next week or so. When teaching this 'send-back', I always throw the dummy in approximately the same place, so that after a week or so the dog gets into the 'habit' of running to this spot for the dummy. It is then a matter of placing the dummy on the spot without him seeing it; then go and get the dog, walk at heel a few paces, point in the direction of the unseen dummy and give

the command 'Go back'. As he has picked this retrieve here many times before he should run out, pick the dummy and return to you: his first blind retrieve. If the dog does not run out to the area of the dummy, it may be necessary to return to allowing him to see you throw the retrieve for a while longer, or you can sit him at the side of the fence with the command 'Stay', then walk forward and place the dummy in the usual area. Walk back to the dog and then send him for the retrieve.

DOUBLE SEND-BACK

Once the dog is confidently running out to the blind retrieve and returning, it is time to place two dummies

Walk the dog away from the dummy, parallel to the fence, for 50 metres or so.

Turn around and give the 'Go back' command.

in the usual area, around 10 metres apart (you don't want him to swap dummies). The dog should be sent to run out and retrieve one dummy; then sit him beside you before sending him back for the second. As usual, give plenty of praise. Repeat the exercise, extending the distance every time it is carried out. When the dog is reliably successful with the two dummy send-back, it is time to start placing the retrieves in different areas of the training field. To start with, let him see you place the dummies, then carry out the send-backs as before, extending the distances gradually over the weeks. The idea behind these exercises is to teach the dog that wherever you point, there will be a dummy there, and it is therefore very important that he is successful and gets encouragement, rather than being shouted at for getting it wrong. If things start to go wrong, it is not the dog's fault – the trainer has taken too big a step too soon. Simply go back and start again, taking smaller steps.

MARKED RETRIEVE WITH A BLIND RETRIEVE

This is another exercise designed to teach the young dog to run out in the required direction to an unseen retrieve. An assistant is required for this exercise. Sit the dog beside you at heel and have your assistant throw a marked retrieve – around 50 metres away is fine. Wait a second or two and send the dog for the retrieve. As soon as he picks it and is on his way back to you, your assistant should place a second dummy in the same spot as the first. When the dog brings

Assistant throwing a marked retrieve.

Assistant placing a second dummy in the same place, unseen to the dog.

the first dummy to hand, send him back to the same area to pick the blind retrieve. This exercise should be repeated as usual, extending the distance and having the dummies thrown across obstacles such as fences or streams and into various cover or crops.

The purpose of the retrieves outlined so far in this chapter is to encourage the young dog to run out confidently in the correct direction, trusting his handler entirely since he has not seen the dummy going out. Therefore, it is very important to give the dog plenty of praise when he gets it right; he should never be scolded if he gets it wrong, as this can cause 'stickiness' on leaving the handler (refusing to leave your sight). The correct action if he fails is to take him back and repeat the exercise, making it shorter and easier until he gets the idea.

TEACHING LEFT AND RIGHT HAND SIGNALS

I tend to start teaching left and right hand signals once the dog is running out confidently for blind retrieves. I start by adding the following exercise onto the end of the training session. As before, a flat grass field should be used initially, and it is helpful to use a fence to assist with the dog taking the correct direction.

To start, sit the dog with his back to the fence, give the command 'Stay' and walk away from him. Just 2 or 3 metres is far enough to start with. Throw a dummy some 15 metres to his left, then take another dummy and throw it to his right. Facing the dog, give the right hand signal along with the command 'Get on'. I find it best to start with the dummy I threw last, as that is the

Throwing the dummy to the left.

Giving the left hand signal, along with the verbal command 'Get on'.

Gradually increase the distance between you and the dog.

one he will tend to want to head for. He should pick the retrieve and deliver it to hand. Give plenty of praise, then sit him back on the spot and repeat the exercise, picking the left hand dummy.

If at any point the dog goes in the wrong direction, stop him on the whistle, and encourage him in the correct direction. When he gets the idea, give him plenty of encouragement and praise. If problems are encountered using the two dummies, it is occasionally necessary to start using just one dummy thrown to the left or right, then give the correct command. After a few days, try again with two dummies, stopping the dog if he gets it wrong.

As usual, over the next few weeks gradually increase the distance of the retrieves to the left and right, till he is confidently running 100 metres or so from his sitting position; at the same time increase your distance from the dog. Eventually, he should be taking left or right commands at 100–150 metres from the handler. It is worth mentioning at this point that while teaching lefts and rights you should alternate which dummy is thrown and in which order the dog is sent for them, as you want the dog to learn the command and not simply to pick up any routine (which they learn very quickly). This is also true with all the disciplines you are teaching the dog; once he learns an exercise, and is carrying out the given command confidently, you should vary the order of the exercise and also the area and terrain you train in. In this way the animal will not get bored and all the time you are reinforcing the given commands, and not simply teaching the dog a routine.

Author's Comment

Dogs learn routines very quickly and easily, and we can make use of this fact in training, initially to teach the commands and then, by changing the order of the routine, to reinforce the command, so the dog is not simply learning a routine.

TEACHING THE 'GO BACK' COMMAND FROM A DISTANCE

This command is used when the dog is searching for a retrieve but is not hunting far enough out. The dog must be stopped using the whistle and hand signal, then given the 'Go back' command along with the appropriate hand signal. This exercise is very easily taught and, as with other handling lessons, should initially take place in a flat grass field where a fence is useful, gradually progressing to various types of terrain and cover, and increasing the distance.

To start, sit the dog beside you at heel. When he has settled, throw a dummy a few metres away parallel to the fence, then, giving the 'Stay' command, walk away from the dog a few metres. Turn around to face him and after a few seconds give the 'Go back' command, whereupon the dog should turn around, run out, pick the dummy and retrieve it to hand. It is quite normal when you start to teach this command for the dog to fail to understand what is required of him; instead of running out for the retrieve, he will come towards you. Simply encourage him to pick the dummy by walking towards it, while repeating both the verbal and hand signals. When he eventually gets the idea, and picks the dummy, give him plenty of praise and repeat the exercise.

Over the next week or so extend the distance that you throw the dummy from the dog, as well as increasing the distance that you walk away from him before turning round and sending him back for the retrieve. When

The correct set-up to teach the 'Go back' command.

Giving the 'Go back' command and the correct reaction from the dog.

this exercise has been thoroughly learned, the next step is to throw the dummy as before, then walk the dog at heel away from the retrieve. About 50 metres or so is fine to begin with. Make him sit with the command 'Stay' and then walk on for a further 50 metres. Then turn around to face the dog and give him the 'Go back' command. As the dog progresses and becomes confident, start taking him to different types of terrain and send him back through cover and across streams and ditches, and so on.

THREE-DUMMY EXERCISE

So far in your Spaniel's directional training you have been teaching your dog to go either left or right as one

Author's Comment

It is important when teaching a young Spaniel to handle that he is successful every time you give a command and he obeys it. In this way the dog will become confident in the handler, so that when you say 'Go back' or 'Get on', he will go in the required direction because he trusts that you are always correct and there will be a dummy where you send him.

The three-dummy exercise.

exercise and to go back as a separate exercise. The next step is to combine these commands using three dummies.

Sit the dog beside you at heel and throw a dummy about 10 metres away, then walk away from the dog, giving the 'Stay' command. About 10 metres or so is plenty at this stage. Face the dog and throw a dummy to his left, at right angles to the first one thrown, and then throw the third dummy to his right; let him settle for a second or two, then give the appropriate hand signal to whichever dummy you want him to pick. It is simpler at this stage to send him for whichever one you threw last, as this is the one he most recently saw and he will naturally want to pick that one. The handler should take the retrieve, giving praise. Sit the dog back on the spot and return the dummy to where it was previously thrown, then walk back and send him for one of the others. When he gets confident and is regularly picking the correct dummy, as in previous exercises, extend the distance of the retrieves and the distance you are from the dog when you give him the directional command. When practising this exercise, you must alternate which dummy you command the dog to pick, from the last one thrown to any of the others. Again the dog is learning the command and not just a routine.

It is time to start practising true blind retrieves when the dog is correctly carrying out all the previous exercises consistently and cleanly. It is best to use light cover to begin with to enable you to see the dog all the way to the dummy. If he heads off in the wrong direction, you can stop him and correct him. He can see you clearly and you can see him. I find it best to hide a few dummies around the chosen area before fetching the dog from the kennel or car; after settling him beside you, carry on and have him pick the retrieves.

When placing the dummies, it is important to take into account the wind direction, in order to avoid the situation where the dog is halfway towards the correct dummy when he catches the scent of another and heads for that one instead. It is advantageous to plant your dummies in completely different areas and walk the dog at heel between them, in this way avoiding the problem altogether. Another factor to take into account when placing dummies, again in regard to wind direction, is that a dog will run out easily when the wind is behind him, but it can be very difficult with a young dog to have him run straight into a head wind. This is because his natural instinct causes him to hunt the wind to pick up scent; he will go left and right but will not go back into the wind because his nose is telling him that there is nothing in front of him to pick. This problem will be overcome later in the dog's training as he gains experience, but for now it is simpler and more convenient to give downwind retrieves. When he has become proficient at downwind retrieves, then on a calm day try him on an upwind retrieve, gradually progressing to windier days. You will be amazed at the difference the wind's strength and direction will make to your dog's handling abilities;

Training Session Exercises

A typical retrieving training session at this point should include the following exercises:

- Walk to heel
- Sit to whistle and stay
- Recall, stopping to whistle halfway
- Recall, straight back to handler
- One long send-back
- One long send-back stopping halfway, then giving the 'Go back' command to pick the dummy
- Two lefts or rights
- A long marked retrieve into light cover, the dog being sent after a suitable delay.

practising in windy conditions as training progresses and the dog becomes more confident is the only way to overcome this problem.

Retrieving the dummies from different situations and types of cover, across streams and walls, and even through hedges should all be practised, gradually increasing the distance of the retrieves.

OVER-HANDLING

There seems to be a tendency among novice trainers to over-handle their dogs. This is detrimental to the dog's efficiency and can become so bad that the dog stops hunting and looks up at the handler for a hand signal. In essence, the dog is then driving the handler, instead of the other way round. To avoid this problem, when the dog is within the approximate area of the retrieve (20 metres or so), he should be left to hunt and to use his natural ability to find the dummy. The handler should only intervene if the dog leaves the area of the fall completely, by stopping the dog and giving the appropriate hand signal to put him back into the right area. Do not try to handle your dog exactly onto the dummy. Instead, put him into the area on the correct side, downwind of the dummy, and let him work it out for himself. In this way you can produce a well trained dog that still maintains all his natural retrieving and hunting ability without becoming robotic and boring to watch.

INTRODUCTION TO SHOT

I would like to start this section by saying that in twenty-five years of training gundogs of all breeds, I have never

Introducing the young Spaniel to the gun by having an assistant throwing dummies and firing shots.

come across one that was truly gun-shy. I have had a few that were nervous of the bang, mostly caused by hapless owners firing shots a metre or so away from the unsuspecting pup, which gets the biggest fright of his short life, and is then naturally suspicious of the object making the infernal racket, i.e. you carrying your gun!

There is a simple and effective method of introducing your dog to shot. Probably the worst tool for this is the starting pistol or dummy launcher, which should never be used. Remember, a dog's hearing is ten to fifteen times more acute than a human's, and I find the sharp crack of a .22 pistol or launcher seems to upset the young dog much more than the 'boom' of a shotgun. The correct method of introducing your dog to the gun is as follows. Have an assistant walk out into an open field some 100–150 metres away from you and your dog. He should be carrying a shotgun, a .410 or 20 bore is ideal, along with a pocket full of light load cartridges and a bag of dummies. Put your young Spaniel on a slip lead and sit him beside you facing your assistant.

When you are ready, ask your assistant to throw a dummy and send your dog to retrieve it. When the dog returns to you, put him back on the leash and have your assistant throw another dummy while simultaneously firing a shot in the air. If your pupil shows any distress, give him praise and let him sit beside you. If you feel he is quite confident, send him for the retrieve, giving plenty of praise on his return. Repeat this as often as is necessary over the next day or two. The next step is to gradually walk towards your dummy-throwing/shot-firing assistant while he throws and shoots. You should stop every 10 metres or so to send the dog for the dummies being thrown. Your dog will soon associate the bang with a dummy being thrown, and the anticipation of the retrieve quickly gets him over any worries he may harbour about the loud bang. Some dogs show absolutely no fear from the start, while others can be very nervous. They are like humans in this respect. Thus, introduction to shot can take half an hour or it can take two weeks: it all depends on the particular dog, but the process cannot be rushed. It also a good idea to take your young Spaniel to a clay pigeon shoot during this time. Starting away at the back, quietly walk around with your dog on a leash, gradually getting closer to the shooting and noise and he will gradually accept this banging as the norm. Your job has been done.

CHAPTER 6

INTRODUCTION TO GAME

This is a very important step in the young Spaniel's training but it is one where many novice trainers slip up badly and many promising young dogs are ruined because the handler has 'lost control'. This is caused by going too fast too soon. Every lesson must be repeated many times for the pupil to digest it properly and for it to become a natural reaction to any given command or situation. It is worth mentioning at this point that any kind of shoot, be it walked up or driven, is definitely not the place to let your pupil see his first pheasant or rabbit. I see many people trying to do just this and it invariably ends with the dog running amok and understandably

An ideal place to start your pupil on game.

so; given the excitement of a shoot day, with many dogs present, coupled with pheasants being flushed and shot, it is a recipe for disaster to try to do any kind of training. Introducing your Spaniel to game must be done gradually, slowly and quietly; by not allowing him to become excited, he will remain obedient.

SUITABLE GROUND

The ideal place to start your pupil on game is a rush field, white grass or frosted bracken, holding a few pheasants or rabbits sitting tight in their forms, as pheasants running in front or rabbits hopping around in plain view is not what you require. There is no need for a gun at this point; in fact, there will be many weeks of hunting and flushing before a gun is necessary. The emphasis of the next few weeks will be on gaining control of the dog, particularly to the turn whistle and stop whistle. The aim is for the dog to flush a sitting rabbit from cover, then sit and watch it run off.

Obviously not everyone has access to a suitable training field, but there are alternatives available. Some professional trainers have rabbit pens which can be rented by the hour; these are very useful as they often contain a few pheasants and partridges too. As you are not shooting the game or rabbits, many landowners and farmers will allow you to train on odd bits of waste ground. There are also many places to train on land with public access and where the rabbits are left mainly unmolested; as long as no laws are broken, you are quite entitled to train your dog there.

HUNTING FOR GAME

Once you have selected your training ground, remember to hunt the dog into the wind to give him the best

A rabbit pen.

chance of contacting game. Don't just take off his leash and let him go hunting. Everything must be done under your control. Sit the dog in front of you and take off his leash along with the command 'Stay'. Let him settle for a few moments before casting him off in the required direction (at right angles to the direction of the wind) with a snap of your fingers and the command 'Get on'. Some 10 or 15 metres is quite far enough for him to travel before you give the turn/recall whistle (two toots), which he must obey instantly and head back towards you, whereupon you give him the command 'Get on' with a snap of the fingers in the opposite direction as you zigzag into the wind, encouraging him to cover the ground properly. It is imperative that you watch your dog very closely when he is hunting up game, because he will tell you when a flush is imminent or

Author's Comment

When handling a Spaniel, or any gundog breed for that matter, the handler must have the whistle in his mouth at all times when the dog is working. If the whistle is dangling around your neck, the few seconds that it takes to get it into your mouth and blow it mean it may as well not be blown at all. The moment will have been lost, and most likely your pupil has hightailed it after his quarry. This is your fault, not the dog's.

Casting the dog off to hunt.

Be ready to stop the dog when the game flushes.

if he has found scent: he will speed up and his tail movement will increase. Through reading your dog's body language, you will be ready when he pushes out his first rabbit, which invariably he will want to chase. It is your job, however, to be ready. The instant that game breaks cover you must blow the stop whistle and give the appropriate hand signal. If earlier training has been successful and thorough, your pupil should sit and watch the rabbit run off or the pheasant fly away. If, however, he takes a few steps after the game before sitting, get hold of him by the scruff of his neck and pull him back to where the rabbit or pheasant flushed, then blow the stop whistle again along with a few sharp words.

After your dog has flushed a rabbit or pheasant and watched it escape, put him back on the leash with plenty of praise just to let him know he has done the correct thing. That is plenty for his first attempt at the 'real thing'. This exercise should repeated two or three times per week if possible or as often as is practical, and in the meantime you should carry on his normal retrieving and obedience training as normal.

It is worth mentioning that running a young Spaniel for too long without a break on your quest for him to contact game can and will have a detrimental effect. He should never be run long enough for him to become tired and slow. A tired dog is never as sharp or obedient as a fresh dog, and you want to maintain a dog with

Author's Comment

The more often your dog is allowed to flush game and then sit and watch it run away without the game being shot or him being sent to retrieve it, the more steady he will become and the chances of him remaining steady will increase dramatically.

speed, drive and style. By running him too long he will begin to pace himself and slow down to a boring pace, thus losing his drive.

So once again, the key is 'little and often'. If after seven or eight minutes of hunting your dog has failed to contact game or flush a bird, call him up, praise him and put him back on the leash. Allow him to rest for twenty minutes or so, letting him have a drink and enabling him to cool down both physically and mentally, then try again, perhaps in a different place where there is more chance of contacting game. When he eventually flushes game, stop him and put him back on the leash as described above.

Personally I find that four or five weeks of flushing and stopping is about right and I never have the game shot until the dog is actually sitting to flush of his own accord and is totally obedient on the turn and stop whistle.

USING PIGEONS

Another method of introducing your young dog to game involves using live homing (or trapped feral) pigeons, which may be ideal for people who do not have access to ground that holds game or rabbits. Some preparation is required for this method, the most obvious requirement being access to pigeons. A rush field or light cover, a roof slate and some string is all that is required, and

Setting up a live pigeon.

Ready to spring the pigeon.

although there are some fancy radio-controlled gadgets on the market, I find the simpler (and cheaper) the better. First, select the piece of ground to be used, then in the middle of the cover dig a small hole just large enough to contain the pigeon, though not so large that the roof slate cannot cover it completely. Attach one end of a piece of string around 10 metres long to the slate, and tie the other end to a metre-long stick, then place the pigeon in the hole and cover it with the slate. Run out the string and place the stick at the end of it some 10 metres away from the slate in an obvious position where you can easily find it. Next, fetch the dog and hunt him upwind towards the pigeon. As soon as he picks up the scent of the bird and goes towards it, simply pull the string and release the pigeon, at the same time blowing the stop whistle and ensuring that the dog sits and watches the bird fly off. The advantage of using this method is that you know exactly where the bird is, thus allowing you to control all the elements of the exercise and to be ready in position to stop the dog when the bird flushes. The disadvantage, apart from

Author's Comment

As your dog is hunting into the wind, it is possible that if he lifts his head, he will scent the pigeon, pheasant or rabbit up to 50 metres or so in front of him, and his natural instinct is to follow up on this; in other words, he will bore straight into the wind towards the source of this 'interesting smell'. This must be discouraged. As soon as it becomes apparent that this is happening, blow the turn/recall whistle and cast him off in the opposite direction. If he persists in following this 'high scent', scold him as he lifts his head and instead make him hunt properly and cover the ground, only allowing him to follow up the scent when he is within 10 or 15 metres or so. A Spaniel's job is to take ground scent to find game, unlike the pointer breeds which hunt air scent and come 'on point' when game is contacted, allowing the handler to get in position before flushing the game.

obtaining sufficient pigeons, is that after repeating the exercise over a few days the dog will begin to anticipate what is going to happen and will stop hunting properly; instead he will watch you, waiting for you to pull the string and release the bird. If this happens, it is then necessary to stop using the captured pigeon method and move on to natural wild game. If you have access to enough birds, it is possible to set out two or three pigeons in a larger area if required.

RETRIEVING GAME

Some dogs will retrieve game readily without any encouragement, while others are not so keen and need

Stopping the dog and pulling the string, allowing the pigeon to flush.

Some young dogs will retrieve game readily.

Most young Spaniels will sniff and examine their first rabbit.

some help to overcome the sensation of feathers or fur in their mouth. Many will mouth the game and lick it but won't pick it up, while others, though retrieving dummies readily to hand, will not pick up a dead rabbit or bird. This in no way reflects on the finished Spaniel's retrieving ability; some of the best retrievers (of all gundog breeds) I have trained were reluctant initially to retrieve their first rabbit. It is necessary to point out at this stage that although I am substituting dummies with cold game (rabbits or birds that have been shot previously), I am still keeping the hunting and retrieving totally separate and teaching the two disciplines on alternate days.

I find the best animals to use for your dog's first retrieve of fur or feather is a half-grown rabbit, shot the previous day and allowed to cool down and stiffen. Dogs find these easier to pick up than freshly shot game. My second choice would be a partridge, again shot previously and allowed to cool. Wood pigeons should be avoided as they are too loose-feathered, while pheasants are too large and awkward for an inexperienced Spaniel to carry. A rabbit, partridge or feral pigeon is a much better option. Game such as this can be frozen for use at a later date (after being thoroughly thawed).

Initially I give the dog a send-back of about 30 metres using a dummy on my everyday training ground, then I repeat the retrieve this time substituting a small rabbit for the dummy. Walk about 30 metres away and then send the dog for the retrieve. On arrival he will sniff the rabbit and, with some encouragement, will pick it up and deliver it to hand, all being well! Unfortunately, this

is not always what happens and some work needs to be done in order to achieve your goal.

PROBLEMS LIFTING GAME AND SOME SOLUTIONS

The first thing to do if your Spaniel fails to lift the rabbit is to walk back and lift the rabbit yourself. Sitting the dog beside you, simply throw the rabbit 10 metres or so and immediately send him for the retrieve; this usually has the desired effect, and with some encouragement he will pick it up and bring it to you.

If this fails, the next step is to 'wind the dog up'.

Placing a dummy in a sock.

Wave the rabbit in front of him and allow him to chase it around you, then throw it, encouraging him to 'run in' and pick it. If success is not forthcoming after three or four attempts, leave it for that day. Give him a retrieve using a dummy, and try again tomorrow. Probably the worst thing you can do is to become frustrated, as the dog will sense this and matters will go from bad to worse. It is much better to put the dog away happy, and try again tomorrow.

If, after a few days, the problem has not resolved itself (it usually does), it is time to try a different approach. Go back to training with dummies for a few days, doing all the usual exercises such as send-backs, rights and lefts, and so on, and do not even try him on cold game. The idea is that he forgets any distaste for a mouthful of fur or feather and enjoys his daily training sessions as before. Then place the dummy inside a thick woollen sock, twisting the end of the sock over and pulling it back down to make a tight, neat little package, and use this instead of a dummy for his training sessions for a few days. When you think the time is right, replace the dummy inside the sock with a cold partridge and carry on his usual daily training. He might sniff the sock before picking it, but familiarity with the sock means he will pick it given some encouragement. The problem of picking game is almost solved. It is then simply a matter of training with this for a few days (using fresh partridges, of course) until he becomes confident of lifting and carrying the sock with the partridge inside. Then he is ready for the final step. Take a sharp knife or scissors and cut a small hole in the sock, and the next day make another, larger hole, until after three or four days you have more hole than sock! You should be able to judge for yourself when the time is right to discard the sock completely and carry on the training programme.

This is a typical example of avoiding trouble or confrontation with your Spaniel. Instead of becoming frustrated and trying to force the animal to retrieve game, simply look at the problem, whatever it is, and approach the training from another angle, producing success and ensuring the dog maintains his confidence and respect for you as his leader.

Over the years I have used the sock method on many Spaniels, Retrievers and HPR (Hunt, Point, Retrieve)

dogs that would not lift game, and it has always, without fail, worked in the end. I have also tried, with varying degrees of success, to attach pheasant or partridge wings to a dummy using gaffer tape, and this can help with some dogs, although personally I find the sock method best.

DAMAGING GAME

It is often the case that some young dogs (and some older ones also), when given a pigeon or rabbit to retrieve for the first time, will mouth the game or pick it up and shake it. I have had dogs that, instead of retrieving it, will try to eat it or pull it apart. This behaviour should of course be discouraged, but it does not mean that the dog is 'hard mouthed', which of course is a major fault with any gundog breed, and the young dog should not be discarded because of it. The young dog, when given a rabbit for his first retrieve, is excited by the scent and feel of the game, but he doesn't really know what he is supposed to do with it. Remember, he is a hunter first and foremost and his instinct probably tells him to eat it, bite it or shake it. We have bred a strong hunting instinct into the animal and also a strong retrieving instinct. In some cases in this situation, the two instincts clash.

The best way of dealing with this is to scold the dog while he is actually mouthing or shaking the rabbit, and immediately encourage him towards you to give up the rabbit. As with all training, timing is all-important: the scold must be instant, and immediately followed by praise and encouragement as he comes towards you. In this way you are teaching him what you require of him. This lesson is normally very quickly learned and the problem overcome. Under no circumstances should you go towards the dog and punish him, for the simple reason that in his mind you are punishing him not for mouthing the game but simply for picking it up. The probable outcome of this is that you put him off retrieving totally, or at the very least discourage him from putting game in his mouth, making your job of producing a useful gundog all the more difficult.

True 'hard mouth' in a gundog is when he consistently damages game by crushing the ribs of the rabbit, partridge or pheasant. This problem can be detected

The correct method of checking game for damage.

by holding the game by its head and feeling the ribcage for damage. If this is the case, then the dog should be discarded as far as gundog training is concerned as this problem is impossible to stop; it is also hereditary, so the dog should never be bred from. However, having said that, a fast, high-flying pheasant that is shot can hit the ground with incredible impact on occasion. Variables such as where the bird landed and what obstacles it hit on the way down must all be taken into consideration when deciding whether the dog damaged the bird or if it was damaged by the impact of the shot or fall. True hard mouth is not that common nowadays in the mainstream working Spaniel breeds, as careful screening and breeding has largely eradicated the problem; if you buy your puppy from field trial lines, this problem is unlikely to arise.

TIME TO MOVE ON

Your dog at this stage should be hunting reliably under control, flushing game and always sitting to the stop whistle. He should also be retrieving cold game/handling out for blind retrieves and delivering the game nicely to hand (*see* Chapter 8). If he is not performing any of these tasks to the required standard, now is the time to go back and carry out more training until the problem is rectified. If not corrected at this stage in the training programme, any such problems will be very difficult to rectify when you bring together the two disciplines of hunting and retrieving. In the next stage the dog will learn 'game sense' and may lose interest in dummies, or in some cases refuse to pick them completely, which is quite understandable once he has had a taste of the real thing. An extra week or two at this stage getting everything right is nothing in comparison to the next twelve years or so of your dog's working life. For example, if your dog 'runs in' (going after a retrieve without being commanded to do so) to retrieve a dummy, there is absolutely no chance of him remaining steady when a large pheasant crashes to the ground 30 metres away. Problems like this need to be sorted out now.

CHAPTER 7

BRINGING IT ALL TOGETHER

At this point in your young dog's training, he should have spent the last few weeks hunting up and flushing game, stopping to flush with the aid of the stop whistle (which with consistency and perseverance will become a habit with the dog and he will eventually drop to flush without the stop command), and watch the game run or fly off. He will be a proficient retriever of dummies and cold game practised on alternate days to hunting and should be obedient to all verbal and hand signals.

In this chapter we are going to teach the Spaniel to hunt up game, flush it, sit steady to shot and retrieve shot game. This is a massive step for the young dog and his first real taste of what being a trained Spaniel is all about. Needless to say, it is also a big step for the novice trainer, as he is at last seeing the result of his efforts over the last eighteen months or so, after rearing the puppy and subsequently training him. However, in your eagerness to see the result, be careful not to overlook some small problem; it is not enough, for example, to just hope that the dog does not run in; if you are in any doubt at all about the dog's obedience, spend

An experienced shooter is required to assist.

another week or two on basic schooling before attempting the next step. The old saying 'two steps forward, one step back' is rarely more appropriate than when applied to gundog training.

It is imperative that over the next week or so you have a reliable assistant to shoot any game flushed by the dog. For obvious reasons he or she should be a proficient and safe shot who is familiar with shooting over dogs if possible. The trainer should never try to shoot the game himself initially, as all his concentration must be on the dog. Even very experienced and successful trainers prefer to have someone else shoot the game for them until the dog gains sufficient experience and can be relied upon to behave in the appropriate manner in all circumstances.

First select a suitable rushy field, hillside or cover, taking into account wind direction and any cover that is likely to hold game. Tell your assistant approximately the direction you will be taking (into the wind), and ask him to walk about 15 metres to your left or right and very slightly behind you to enable him to see exactly where you and your dog are at all times. This is especially important when shooting rabbits to avoid any possibility of an accident. Also ask him not to shoot unless the dog is sitting steadily, and to let the game out some 25–35 metres before firing; you do not want the game landing too close to the dog as this would put too much temptation in his way and increase the possibility of a run-in, which at all costs you must avoid.

Cast your dog off as normal and quarter him across the wind, taking plenty of time to allow him to hunt the ground and explore any likely places in front of you where a rabbit or pheasant could be hiding. With luck, the dog will contact game fairly quickly, and by this time you should have gained enough experience to be able to 'read' your dog and know when a flush is imminent. When this occurs, immediately warn your assistant to get ready so he is prepared to take a shot when the game bolts or takes flight. You, on the other hand, must be focused entirely on the dog. The instant the game flushes, be ready with the stop whistle and

Your dog will run in when you least expect it.

hand signal to ensure that the dog sits while the pheasant flies off.

As you will discover, it is very difficult not to take your eyes off the dog for a second to watch the pheasant or rabbit being shot, but you *must* concentrate as this is exactly the moment when your dog will decide to run in, and if your attention is elsewhere, the moment will be lost. With luck, this will not happen and your aspiring gundog will sit perfectly, whereupon plenty of praise should be given and the dog put back on the leash.

Pick the pheasant or rabbit by hand for the first two or three shots as this teaches the dog that not everything shot is for him to retrieve and that he only gets to retrieve when commanded to do so.

As I have said previously in this book, dogs pick up habits extremely quickly, and therefore if you allow your Spaniel to pick and retrieve the first three or four birds or rabbits that it has seen shot, he will assume that any game flushed on his beat is to be retrieved. This is exactly what you do not want, as running-in is the next step! Once started, it is very difficult to stop reliably. Remember, your dog will retrieve now until the day he dies, but he will only remain trained and steady for as long as you keep him that way. You must instil in the young Spaniel the habit of watching game fly off and being shot before you allow him his first retrieve of the game he has flushed.

FIRST FIND AND RETRIEVE

After the pheasant he has flushed has been collected, walk the dog on the leash away from the area of the first shot; 30 or 40 metres should suffice. Sit him in front of you and cast him off to carry on hunting for more game. Two flushes and shots are about right for his first outing. If your pupil has remained steady to flush and shot, and you are satisfied that he has now gained the habit of being steady, it is now time for his first retrieve.

When game is flushed, ensure that your Spaniel is sitting steadily.

I allow a young Spaniel to retrieve every second rabbit or pheasant it flushes. This helps to maintain steadiness.

As before, have your dog hunting in front of you and your assistant beside you when game is flushed and is shot. Ensure the dog is sitting steadily and the game has been cleanly killed. Walk over to the dog, point him in the required direction and give him the 'Go back' command. Handle him out to pick the game as normal. Do not be in too much of a hurry to send him for the retrieve; it is far better to take a few minutes just to let the dog settle and cool down mentally before sending him. If all your training so far has been successful, he will pick the rabbit and retrieve it to hand. Typically I would allow a young Spaniel from this stage onwards to retrieve every second rabbit or pheasant that he flushes; in this way the dog is gaining necessary experience while still maintaining steadiness and overall obedience.

RUNNERS

Runners are shot birds that have not been killed cleanly and have run off wounded. As a general rule, I would not send a young dog in his first few outings to collect a runner; it is much better to allow him to gain some experience picking dead game for a while before letting him follow up the scent of a wounded bird. If this happens during training, the easiest solution is to have your assistant shoot the bird again while it is on the ground and before it has a chance to gather itself and run off. Alternatively, have an older dog to hand to retrieve any game that is wounded.

In the past I have seen dogs that would readily pick runners but refuse to pick a dead pheasant, the reason being that they have been allowed to pick too many runners far too soon. Another practice that I see all too often at shoots, be it driven or walked up, is shooters sending their dogs to chase after pheasants that have been shot and wounded and are running off in full view across a flat grass or stubble field. This is a big mistake; instead of seeing good gundog work, in other words the dog using its nose to find the scent of the fallen bird and following the trail until it can pick and retrieve, a simple chase occurs, with the dog racing after the running bird around the field by sight, probably joined by two or three other dogs which have decided to join in the fun. The correct course of action is to allow the game to reach cover, then send the Spaniel to the fall (the point where the wounded bird landed), allowing him to pick up the scent, follow it and retrieve the bird to hand. This is proper gundog work and is a joy to watch.

WORKING IN COMPANY

Shooting is a social sport and as such is usually practised in company with other like-minded people and their dogs, all out to enjoy their day. In contrast, dog training on the whole tends to be a solitary business

Never send your young dog to retrieve a running pheasant in the open, as the result will simply be a chase instead of good gundog work.

Having more dogs and handlers present when training allows the young Spaniel to gain experience.

with many hours spent with just you and your dog. It should come as no surprise, therefore, after training your dog all summer and autumn more or less undisturbed, that come October and the first shoot of the season your young Spaniel behaves totally out of character, chasing after other dogs, ignoring commands and generally acting as if he had never been trained at all. On the other hand, he may be nervous and frightened of everything and everybody, heading back to the vehicle at any opportunity. Such reactions to his first outing in company are perfectly normal unless some preparatory training and gradual socialization is given. Put yourself in your dog's position: the poor creature has never seen so many other dogs and probably didn't think there were so many people in the whole world. To expect him to behave as he does normally at home is asking too much and it just won't happen.

When you are confident that your dog is performing correctly and can be relied upon to flush the game, sit steadily and then retrieve on command, then another trainer and his dog should be introduced. This is quite a big step and you will probably find that your pupil pays too much attention to the other dog or handler. This is perfectly normal, and given time he will settle down and get on with the job. Obviously the other dog must be well trained and the handler experienced to enable the training/shooting session to run smoothly. The dogs and handlers should be around 20 metres apart, with the shooters positioned between them and everyone moving slowly in the same direction, which will allow the Spaniels to cover their respective beats properly, minimizing the possibility of missing game. Both dogs should be hunting at the same time under control and obeying the whistle commands of their handlers until

'Leave That!'

For example: my Spaniel flushes a rabbit and the rabbit is shot, falling dead in full view just a few metres from the dog. To allow the dog to retrieve this rabbit to hand would teach him nothing new and would only serve to excite him unnecessarily. Thus I give the command 'Leave that', call him to heel and walk away from the rabbit. A few paces away I sit him in front of me and cast him off to carry on hunting for more game, leaving the shot rabbit to be picked as a 'blind' retrieve later on. If another rabbit is shot soon after, I tell him to 'Leave that', turn around and send him back for the first rabbit.

Tell him to 'Leave that' and cast him off in the opposite direction.

A Spaniel hunting gorse/whin.

game is flushed and shot. The idea is to alternate the retrieves between the dogs, which also teaches your young dog to sit steadily and watch the other dog retrieving without whining or interfering in any way with the other dog's efforts. During this time, while the other handler and his dog are picking the game, you must concentrate on your own dog, watching and waiting for him to make a move and being prepared to blow the stop whistle and scold him and return him to the spot where he was told to stay. Your dog will soon get the idea and realize he must not move while his brace mate is retrieving. As you and your dog become more experienced it will become possible to invite three or four handlers and their dogs to participate in a training session, along with another shooter or two, which will increase the chance of having dead game on the ground to retrieve. This process gradually increases the experience of the young dog, while enabling you to insist that he remains obedient. This is imperative for producing a useful Spaniel.

GAINING EXPERIENCE

This is probably the most interesting and satisfying part of training a young Spaniel as you are seeing all your efforts come to fruition. However, dogs are not machines and if you don't keep up his training and stretch his abilities, both hunting and retrieving, his potential will never be met. I find the best and easiest way to do this is to train on different terrain every outing. Some days have the game shot that he flushes, other days making him sit as the birds fly off. I like to train in areas where there is an abundance of rabbits sitting in suitable cover, as this gives unlimited scope to shoot rabbits and to set up and practise situations that can arise during actual shoots.

A spaniel hunting forest brash.

A Spaniel hunting heather.

In this way you are making the best use of any game that is shot. As the training progresses, you can extend the distances and the difficulty of the retrieves. It is also very important to allow the dog to hunt as well as to retrieve in as much variation of cover as possible. There is unlimited scope for this, a few examples are: gorse/whin, bramble bushes, forest brash, nettles, rashes, frosted bracken, standing bracken, willowherb and heather.

Dogs react differently in different types of cover, and it is my experience that rabbits and pheasants behave differently depending on what type of cover they are in. For example, rabbits tend to sit very tight in heather, whereas in gorse or standing bracken they are apt to run more freely. The dog and trainer must learn this – and the only way is to get out there and practise in as many different situations as possible.

PEGGING

As your Spaniel gains experience, he will sooner or later learn to 'peg' (catch un-shot game), which is obviously a fault in a gundog. Some dogs become expert at this if left unchecked. Many years ago I had an English Springer Spaniel called Ben, who became so adept at 'pegging' that the guns rarely got a shot. On one occasion I was flushing rabbits with Ben at a retriever training day run by John Halsted Snr of Drakeshead Kennels, and within half an hour John had nicknamed my dog 'The Grim Reaper'. This was very funny at the time but is a good example of how leaving a problem unsolved means it only gets worse and worse. There are a few instances when your Spaniel will peg game through no fault of yours or your dog's, for instance rabbits with myxomatosis. These will not run or even move in some instances, and the young Spaniel will just lift them and carry them back to you. Another example is young pheasants which can't or won't fly; the dog, smelling the pheasants, goes to investigate and simply picks them up. When this happens, or if he lifts a healthy un-shot rabbit or pheasant, the same course of action applies. Simply stop the dog using the stop whistle and don't allow him to retrieve it to you. Instead, go towards the Spaniel and take the rabbit gently from him, giving the command 'Leave that'; then put the rabbit down in full view of the dog and allow it to run off unmolested. If you are consistent in this, the young Spaniel very quickly learns not to catch un-shot game, and begins to differentiate between the smell of game that has been shot and game that hasn't. One is a mixture of gunpowder residue and blood, the other purely the scent of rabbit or pheasant.

Spaniels can be trained to become very adept at differentiating between shot and un-shot game. I have owned Spaniels that would 'go in' with their feet stamping the ground, trying to flush a pheasant or rabbit that would not move.

CHAPTER 8

COMMON PROBLEMS AND SOLUTIONS

DELIVERY

The delivery is the act of the dog handing over the dummy or shot game to the handler. I have deliberately left this topic until this stage of training, as more often than not any problem with delivery will sort itself out as the dog gains confidence and experience.

However, on some occasions it does not and the problem needs to be addressed. I have trained many different breeds of gundog over the years and found

A good delivery.

A bad, untidy delivery.

that Spaniels on the whole are quite difficult to teach to give a good delivery in comparison with Retrievers or HPRs. The latter seem to want to give me the dummy and sit properly in front, lifting their head as if to say 'Here, take it'. Many Spaniels on the other hand will drop the dummy at your feet, or when they are still 10 or 20 metres away from the handler. Some will come right in, drop the dummy and lie on it, while others will just do anything to avoid giving up the retrieve, squirming around and rolling on their backs. Of course, I am speaking generally and there are exceptions to

every rule, and some Spaniels will naturally give perfect deliveries without any work from the trainer. However, in my experience most will not – it has to be taught. When the puppy is very young and you roll a tennis ball for him to retrieve to you, it is very important not to just take the ball and praise him. Instead, let him hold the ball for a time, giving lots of praise while you rub his neck, face and head. This encourages the puppy to hold on to the ball and gives him confidence that you are not going to simply take it from him. By carrying on in this way throughout the Spaniel's training, many of

Let the young dog hold the ball, while you rub his head, neck and face, giving lots of praise.

the difficulties in delivery can be avoided. You can take it a step further with an older puppy, so that you always touch his head before giving the command 'Leave' and remove the dummy gently from his mouth.

Putting pressure on a young dog to give up his retrieve properly can on occasions put him off retrieving completely. Obviously this is the last thing you would want to happen. I find that it is far better to leave any delivery problems until the dog is fully trained or until I can stand it no longer.

Problem 1: The dog drops the dummy 10 metres or so from the handler and returns without the dummy.

This is the most common problem and is usually caused by the novice trainer pulling the dummy out of the dog's mouth as it runs past him. This hurts the dog:

Always touch his head as you take the dummy.

the dummy weighs around a pound and the dog has to grip it with reasonable force in order to carry it. Having it ripped out of his mouth as he attempts to run past the trainer is painful, and being an intelligent animal he decides never to go near the trainer carrying a dummy again. The more you try to encourage him towards you, the further back he will drop it.

To resolve this problem you must teach the dog that no pain is produced by being in close proximity to you, and give him confidence that he is doing the correct thing. The correct method of teaching this takes a week or so of daily ten-minute lessons. With the dog on a leash attached to a fence, place him in a sitting position. Kneel down level with him and place the dummy in his mouth, giving the command 'Hold', and then praise him while rubbing his neck and head,

A dog dropping the dummy before reaching the handler is usually caused by the novice trainer snatching the dummy from his mouth as he runs past.

Teaching the dog to hold the dummy on command.

Using the corner of a field to guide the Spaniel into the correct position.

Apply gentle but increasing pressure to his foot as you give the 'Leave' command, until he releases his grip.

making sure he keeps hold of the dummy. He may try to spit it out, in which case return the dummy gently to his mouth repeating the 'Hold' command while giving plenty of praise. He will eventually get the idea and hold the dummy in your presence.

A few days' repetition of this is all that is required before going on to the next step. Have the dog on a leash beside you and encourage him to carry the dummy while walking at heel. If he drops it, scold him immediately and replace the dummy in his mouth, giving the 'Hold' command and plenty of praise. When he has learned this lesson and is carrying the dummy reliably at heel, you can move on to the next step. Throw a marked retrieve and send him for it, but as soon as he picks the dummy, walk away from him in the opposite direction. As he gets closer, tell him to 'Heel' without looking round, and carry on walking. Allow him to carry the dummy for a minute or two before rubbing his head and giving the 'Leave' command. Carry on with this for as long as is necessary to reprogramme the dog so he is happy carrying a dummy in his mouth around you.

Problem 2: The dog drops the dummy at your feet.

This problem can be cured in exactly the same way as Problem 1, and in fact is much simpler to put right using this method.

Problem 3: The dog runs past you with the dummy and circles around you.

Ideally, the dog should come straight to you, then sit or stand to give you the retrieve. Unfortunately, most of them want to skirt around you for a while before giving up the retrieve. A simple and effective way of dealing with this is to stand with a fence behind you, so that when the dog returns to you, he cannot run past or circle you. Using the corner of a field is even better, as the right angle of the fence guides the dog into the correct position. A week to ten days or so is normally enough time to stop the dog's bad habit of running past you, and he should now be reliably coming straight up to you as is correct.

Problem 4: The dog grips the dummy or game and won't release it.

This is another very common problem in young dogs. I am astonished at the number of handlers I see regularly tearing the game out of the dog's mouth while I am judging Retriever trials. It is even worse with many Spaniel handlers. It looks very bad and there is absolutely no reason to continue this practice as it is very quick and simple to correct.

First, the dog must be taught to come straight in with the dummy and to sit in front of the handler correctly. Stroke his head and give the command 'Leave' as you take the dummy in your other hand. If the dog refuses to let go, use your foot to apply gentle but increasing pressure to his paw until he releases his grip and you can remove the dummy; then give him plenty of praise. It normally only takes a few sessions for the dog to learn the 'Leave' command, although it may be necessary to repeat the lessons using cold game, then again with freshly shot game.

Problem 5: The dog comes in to the handler but lies down holding the dummy.

When faced with this problem, the first thing I do is to refuse to bend down to take the retrieve from the dog. Instead, I encourage the dog to sit up towards me by patting my chest and giving the 'Hup' command. This usually works. If you consistently refuse to accept a retrieve while the dog is lying down, he will eventually come straight in to you, sit up and give you the dummy.

RUNNING IN

A dog is said to 'run in' when he goes to collect a retrieve without being sent by the handler.

This is probably the most common problem I am asked to resolve. The best advice I can give is never to let it happen in the first place. It is caused entirely by the novice trainer skipping over the basics because he is so keen to get on to the more advanced training. But there are no short cuts in training a Spaniel. If the basics have not been properly instilled in the dog as training progresses, problems such as running in will appear. However, there are some steps you can take which will help to resolve the issue. To start with, no further retrieves should be allowed until the Spaniel is completely steady to first dummies, then cold game and finally freshly shot game. I prefer to take the

Encourage the dog to sit up with the dummy by refusing to take it from him while he is lying down.

dog right back to stage one, where he is back on the check chain and expanding leash, this time concentrating on instilling steadiness over and above everything else.

Steadiness Exercises

These exercises should be carried out in the order given here.

Exercise 1: While walking along with the dog on a leash at heel, throw a dummy, at the same time snapping the check chain and blowing the stop whistle. Leave the dog sitting while you collect the dummy. This should be repeated many times over the period of a week or more if required, until the dog sits automatically when a dummy is thrown.

Exercise 2: With your Spaniel on the check chain and extending leash, allow him to hunt in front of you.

After a minute or so blow the stop whistle and throw the dummy 30 metres or so away from the dog. Giving the 'Stay' command, leave the dog (I just drop the extending leash with the trigger locked on the ground) and collect the dummy yourself. Again, this should be repeated until you are satisfied that the lesson has been thoroughly learned.

Exercise 3: Repeat the previous two exercises but introduce the use of a starting pistol shot when the dummy is in the air. Again full attention must be paid to the dog sitting steadily while you pick the retrieve.

Exercise 4: Replace the dummy with cold game and repeat exercise 3.

Exercise 5: Unclip the extending leash from the check chain. When the dog is hunting in front of you, blow the stop whistle and throw the cold game (pigeon or rabbit) before picking by hand.

Walking the dog at heel while throwing dummies and picking them yourself teaches the dog steadiness.

Throwing dummies while the dog is hunting.

Throwing dummies in conjunction with a shot.

Throwing cold game in conjunction with a shot.

Exercise 6: At this stage an assistant is required to shoot rabbits or pigeons as the trainer's attention needs to be fully on the dog. Ferreting rabbits and/or decoying wood pigeons are excellent methods for teaching steadiness. It is obviously imperative that the Spaniel is not allowed to retrieve any of the game shot, until the handler is fully satisfied that the dog is now steady and will not run in.

Exercise 7: When ferreting or decoying, and the dog has sat steadily while three or four rabbits or pigeons have been shot, pick most of them by hand, leaving one for the dog to retrieve. Go back to him and send him for the last rabbit or pigeon.

These exercises reprogramme the Spaniel to be steady to shot and fall of game. It is important that the trainer gives lots of encouragement and praise if the dog sits correctly when game is shot, and chastises him instantly if he shows any sign of moving without being commanded to do so. In order that the dog remains steady, he must only be allowed to pick one out of every two or three rabbits, pheasants or whatever is being shot.

CHASING GAME

This is when the dog hunts correctly but when he flushes game, instead of sitting immediately and allowing it to be shot, he gives chase. Again, this problem arises because the basic stop whistle command has not been taught properly. The way I deal with this problem is similar to the method described in the previous section on running in.

First, the dog must be taught to sit immediately to the stop whistle, in any situation and under any circumstances, using the check chain and flexi lead. Once this is instilled into the dog, you can progress onto flushing rabbits from rushes or using a rabbit pen if possible. As soon as the rabbit moves, a tug on the chain combined with the blown whistle command to stop the dog should be given. When the dog sits, give him praise and then carry on hunting in the opposite direction from where the flushed rabbit ran off. If the Spaniel moves during these exercises, even a little way, he must be chastised and returned to the place where the rabbit was flushed from, as you repeatedly blow the stop whistle.

Through consistency and many days of repetition you can reprogramme the Spaniel to sit to flush instead of chasing. Once you are confident that your pupil has learned the lesson, simply unclip the chain from the flexi lead and carry on hunting as normal.

Author's Comment

In this chapter, as well as in previous chapters, I have used the phrase 'unclip the check chain from the flexi lead'. I would like to explain the importance of this, as opposed to removing the check chain from the dog's neck. While training with the chain and flexi, you are in complete control. The dog knows this and will obey all commands instantly. However, removing the chain from his neck tells him he is free, and with some dogs all lessons can be instantly forgotten. To avoid this problem, I have found by experience that it is possible to unclip the leash from the chain without the dog even noticing the transition. He will obey commands and behave in the same way as he would if the flexi was still connected because he still feels the loose chain around his neck. By intermittently having him on and off the flexi at various stages throughout any training session, the dog will learn to obey any given command whether he is connected physically to the trainer via the flexi or not.

In this chapter I have listed a few of the most common problems that can arise while training a Spaniel (or most other gundogs for that matter), and the methods I use to rectify them. However, it would be impossible to list every possible problem as new ones arise with every dog I train. The skill in training any dog is to see the start of a problem arising and to work out a strategy for rectifying the problem before it becomes a habit, which is then much more difficult to put right. Again I cannot stress enough the importance of training the young Spaniel properly and thoroughly from the start, making sure he has absorbed each step of training completely before moving to the next step. By taking time and being patient you will avoid the problems listed in this chapter and you will find it a very straightforward and simple process to produce a well trained Spaniel of whom you can be proud.

CHAPTER 9

ADVANCED RETRIEVING AND WATER WORK

Many sportsmen are more than happy simply to own a Spaniel which behaves well, hunts within range of the gun and retrieves game to hand when commanded to do so. However, if you have enjoyed training and working with your dog, why stop there? Your dog has the ability to learn and become adept at so much more, for example, handling out to blind retrieves up to 200 metre or more, crossing rivers, lakes and anything else that stands in his way. The summer months are fantastic for teaching advanced work; after all, come February the Spaniel is redundant as far as work on shoots is concerned. They are such active little dogs it is a shame to just leave them in the kennel when they are able and willing to be taught to a very high standard of retrieving

During a send-back, I occasionally stop the dog halfway and give him the 'Go back' command.

on land or water – and they just love it! When I take my own dogs near a pond or lake in warm weather they will spend ages swimming around looking for something to retrieve. It's so much better to give a dog a reason to be in there and learning new skills, if for no other reason than that you can, and he is willing.

When teaching a Spaniel any type of advanced water work, it is obviously impossible to get out to the dog (unless you enjoy swimming). It is therefore imperative that the dog is thoroughly taught directional hand signal and stop whistle commands on land before attempting to teach him to handle on water. For this reason I discuss advanced retrieving first and advanced water work later in the chapter.

ADVANCED RETRIEVING

Exercise 1: Getting him out to distance.

Spaniels get used to working within a certain distance of the handler (which is normally as far as you can throw a dummy). They will run out 40 or 50 metres or so and start hunting, looking for the dummy at the distance it is normally at. To teach a dog to get out further I use send-backs, where I initially let the dog see the dummy thrown, and then walk away for ever-increasing distances before sending him back for the retrieve. I do the same over fences and rivers, occasionally stopping the dog halfway and then giving him the 'Go back' command.

When the dog has gained enough confidence to run out long distances, I start placing two or three dummies in the same area and repeatedly send him to that area from varying starting points to pick one of the dummies. The key to success here is the dog having confidence in the handler; he must trust that when you point him in any direction and say 'Go back', there is a dummy there to be picked. The only way to gain the dog's confidence is through his success and subsequent praise when he gets it right. Repeat the above exercise in different places, over varying terrain and across obstacles.

Giving the left hand command at distance.

Alternate between picking the game immediately and leaving it to be retrieved later.

Exercise 2: Teaching left and right commands at distance.

The dog taking perfect left or right commands at 40 or 50 metres from the handler is one thing, but it is quite another when he is 200 metres away. However, with practice it is perfectly feasible to teach this. I use a long (100 metres or so) send-back, letting the dog see the dummy being placed. Unseen to the dog, I then place a second dummy 20 or 30 metres to the right or left of the line the dog will take on his way out for the seen dummy. Send him for the dummy, and when he comes level with the unseen dummy, stop him and give the left or right command to guide him towards the unseen dummy. It may be necessary to stop the dog a few times and redirect him as he will be keen to run back for the first (seen) dummy. This exercise teaches the dog to have confidence in you and to trust that when you give a command, be it 'Left', 'Right' or 'Go back', there is always a retrieve there to be picked. When the dog has become reliable at taking the left or right hand signal, simply increase the distance of the first dummy thrown and set the unseen dummy further back, and also further from the line the dog will take.

It is very important, as with any training, to vary the retrieve between allowing him to pick the first dummy and stopping him and giving the left or right command to find the unseen dummy. If you do not do this, he will begin to anticipate being stopped and will not run out the distance.

Exercise 3: Teaching distance work while shooting rabbits or walking up game.

As your dog becomes more proficient at hunting up, flushing and retrieving game shot for him, an excellent method of giving him more challenging retrieves while walking up rabbits or game is to leave the shot/dead rabbit or pheasant lying where it was shot and allow him to carry on hunting for more game to be shot. When you are at a more challenging distance, or have manoeuvred so that there are some obstacles or cover between you and the retrieve, send the dog for the retrieve and handle him out to the rabbit or pheasant. Care should be taken again to alternate between picking the game immediately and leaving it to be retrieved

later, to avoid the possibility of the dog anticipating your next command.

Exercise 4: Handling the Spaniel through or across a blind valley or cover (where the dog cannot see the handler and the handler cannot see the dog).

This is a problem often encountered while shooting or training on the edge of grouse moors and rough ground. The game may fall, for example, on the opposite side of a deep gulley, often with a stream or deep bracken at the bottom, making it very difficult to handle the dog out to the other side as the handler cannot see the dog hunting at the bottom. This situation can be set up easily and the solution practised until the Spaniel becomes proficient at taking verbal and whistle commands out of sight of the handler.

First, select a suitable area for training, such as a steep-sided gulley or similar. With the dog sitting in the bottom of the gulley, throw a dummy over his head and up the banking some 40 metres or so, then turn around and walk up the opposite bank, leaving the dog sitting in the bottom. Walk far enough that you are just out of sight. Then turn around and give the verbal 'Go back' command. More often than not the dog will just sit there, as he is used to seeing a hand signal in conjunction with the verbal command 'Go back'. It may be necessary to go to the lip of the slope and give a hand signal, but after a few tries he will get the idea and head up the slope to pick the retrieve. Once the dog becomes proficient at this, place a blind retrieve across the gulley, then fetch the dog and handle him across to it. He may well 'stick' in the bottom, in which case blow the stop whistle and give the 'Go back' command, whereupon the dog should, given practice, appear on the other side of the gulley.

This exercise should be practised in a variety of hollows and gulleys, with various obstacles such as streams, rivers, bracken or rashes. The object of the exercise is to be able to push your dog through any terrain to get him to the dummy. You can then practise in pairs on shot game or rabbits, by having a Spaniel and a handler with a gun on each side of the gulley, flushing game and swapping retrieves.

Giving the 'Go back' command with the dog unseen in the bottom of a gulley.

Exercise 5: Teaching the Spaniel to 'Hold an area'.

Some species of game can be very difficult to pick on occasion, especially snipe, and in some conditions partridges and woodcock. This is due mainly to poor scenting conditions preventing the scent of the shot bird from spreading upwards and outwards. If the dog can't smell the bird, he cannot possibly pick it. To give him the best chance of smelling the bird, it is sometimes necessary to handle the Spaniel very close to the 'fall' and to keep him in that area, hunting thoroughly and not just running through because his nose is telling him there is nothing there. On many occasions I have seen dog after dog fail to pick dead partridges lying in a perfectly flat harrowed field. The bird is there in full view, lying belly down, and it seems the dog is bound to pick it. But as no scent is rising, the dog will fail unless the handler is capable of handling the dog right onto the target.

To teach a dog to hold a tight area while hunting, I use the verbal command 'There, there' repeatedly, while giving a hand signal similar to bouncing a ball. First, select an area of light cover; white grass or frosty bracken is ideal for this purpose. Sit the dog and let him see you place a tennis ball deep into the cover around a metre in front of him. Tell the dog to 'Stay' as you walk away from him (around 20 metres is plenty initially), then turn around to face him and give him the 'There, there' command along with the hand signal encouraging him to put his nose down to find the tennis ball and retrieve it to you. After a few attempts he will get the idea.

The next stage is to hide the tennis ball. Then fetch your dog. As before, sit him a metre or so behind the ball, then walk away for 20 metres or so before turning around and giving the 'There, there' command. This lesson normally only takes a day or two for the

Teaching the 'There, there' command.

dog to learn. It is then a simple matter of extending the distance and varying the cover in which you hide the ball. Many Spaniels will not hunt if there is no cover or scent, so it is a good idea to use a flat grass field on occasions; by pushing the ball into the grass it can be hidden from the dog's view. Finally, when the dog has become adept at carrying out this exercise, I place two or three tennis balls in different locations around the training field, standing them deep into cover. Then I get the dog and handle him out towards a particular ball; when he is in the correct position, I stop him and give the 'There, there' command.

As with other training, success is important in teaching the Spaniel this exercise. However, by making the retrieve easier to begin with and only gradually hiding the ball in more difficult places, he will be successful and learn the command.

ADVANCED WATER WORK

A Spaniel that handles well in water is very impressive to watch; more importantly, it is very useful in the field. Often someone shoots a duck or pheasant that lands on or across water, unseen to the dog. I find teaching dogs to handle in water really enjoyable and satisfying, especially in the summer months when the dogs seem to love being in the water and are keen to get back in time after time.

The first subject I am going to discuss regarding water is the delivery. When a dog exits the water carrying a dummy, the first thing he wants to do is to drop the retrieve on the ground and shake himself dry. This is a fault, whether he picks it up again and brings it to you or not. If he is carrying a wounded pheasant or duck, the moment the dog drops the bird it will run off, possibly never to be found again. This is unacceptable.

During the early stages of training in water the handler must be right at the edge of the pond or river, meeting the dog as soon as it exits the water, even standing in the water to start with. This allows the dog neither time nor distance to drop the dummy and shake. This can become a habit and difficult to stop. It is much simpler not to allow the practice to happen in the first place by standing right on the edge of the water. As soon as the dog emerges, bend down and put your hand on the top of his head (he can't shake if you are putting slight pressure on his head), take hold of the dummy with your other hand and then give the 'Leave' command. Stand clear or you will get wet!

As training progresses, stand slightly further back from the water with each retrieve until after a week or so he will not drop the dummy and shake. If, during this time he does drop it, scold him instantly and return the dummy to his mouth, encouraging him to carry it to you before shaking.

WATER EXERCISES

Exercise 1: Send-back into pond or lake.

I like to start off by giving the dog a straight marked retrieve into the water from about 10 metres from the edge of the pond, just to get him in the mood. Following

The dog should not drop the dummy to shake before delivery.

A good delivery from water.

on from this, I throw a marked retrieve back into the same place, this time turning around and walking the dog at heel away from the pond for about 30 metres; this is quite far enough to begin with. Sit the dog, then send him for the retrieve. I make every subsequent send-back slightly further and more difficult. After a few sessions, when he is running out and entering the water confidently, I occasionally stop the dog using the whistle at the edge of the water and then give the 'Go back' command, which teaches him to enter water at a distance when commanded to do so.

Exercise 2: Blind retrieve in water with a distraction thrown.

This is taught in a similar way to Exercise 1, with the addition of a marked retrieve being thrown to the left or right of the dog and handler before sending the dog back for the dummy in the water. To begin with, throw a dummy well out into the pond while the dog sits beside you. Turn around and walk the dog at heel a good distance away from the pond. Sit the dog and throw a long marked retrieve at 90 degrees to the line the dog will take to the pond and the first dummy thrown. Turn

Teaching a dog to enter water at a distance from his handler.

away from the marked retrieve, giving the command 'No', and send him back for the one in the water. When he retrieves the first dummy send him to pick the mark, giving lots of praise on his return. It is possible to make these retrieves more difficult by going further from the water and closing the angle of the distraction thrown. When the dog has become proficient at this, the next step is to throw the dummy in the water unseen to the dog and repeat the exercise. He is now performing a blind retrieve in water with a marked distraction.

Exercise 3: Blind retrieve across water.

When teaching a Spaniel across water, it is best to start training on a river rather than a pond. When the

dog exits the water on the other side and picks the dummy, he will try to come back to you by running around the pond rather than re-entering the water and swimming directly back, which is the correct way of doing this. If a river is used initially, this problem can be avoided. You may think this is nit-picking, but it is much simpler to start off correctly than to have to rectify a problem later. The reason why the dog should not go round the pond is quite obvious: it may disturb ground that has not yet been hunted and may flush game too far out for the handler to shoot: an opportunity missed!

First, throw a marked retrieve across the river and send the dog to pick it. If successful, throw the dummy back in the same place, and walk back from the river's

Dog sitting while a distraction is thrown.

The dog is then sent to pick the blind retrieve.

edge some 50 metres or so with the dog at heel, then turn around and send him back across the river to pick the retrieve. When he returns with the dummy give him loads of praise and repeat the exercise a few times, extending the distance between the edge of the river and where you send him from. Two or three retrieves per session is quite sufficient, as giving him more can sicken the dog and put him off, especially if the water is cold.

Once the dog is proficiently crossing the water, hunting the far bank and retrieving the dummy to hand, change the exercise by stopping the dog before he enters the water and giving the 'Go back' command, whereupon he should turn around, enter the water and cross to find the dummy and return it to hand. Give loads of praise. When he has learned this and is taking the 'Go back' command reliably from a distance, prac-

tise stopping him when he is two-thirds of the way across the water, and then give him the 'Go back' command. He should carry on across the water and exit on the far bank, pick the retrieve and return it to hand. Remember that when stopping a dog using the whistle command in water, it is obviously impossible for the dog to stop swimming, as he would sink. However, he should be expected at the very least to turn around and look at you, waiting for a directional command.

Exercise 4: Left and right commands in water.

All the water retrieves I have explained so far in this chapter have involved encouraging the dog to go back in or across water. It is also necessary to be able to handle the dog to either left or right while he is swimming. It is impossible to teach the dog left and right

Teaching the dog to exit on the far bank.

Re-entering the water with the dummy.

Giving the 'Stop' command in water, followed by the 'Go back' command.

Teaching left and right commands in the water.

commands in water using the same method as used on land. Instead, throw two dummies into the pond around 30 metres apart and send the dog to fetch one; he will invariably head for the last one thrown. Wait until he is halfway towards the dummy and then blow the stop whistle. When he turns around and looks at you, give him a left or right hand signal guiding him to pick the other dummy. It may be necessary to stop him more than once to redirect him to the dummy you want him to pick, rather than the last one he saw thrown. As his handling in water improves, more than two dummies can be used, practising handling him from one dummy to another.

The most important thing when teaching any dog water work is knowing when to stop. Spaniels especially can get very cold if given too many retrieves in any one training session. It is much better to give him

a few retrieves in water first and then do some hunting, which allows him to warm up and dry off before heading for home. A cold and/or tired dog will become unresponsive and disobedient, turning the training session into a fiasco with both dog and trainer becoming frustrated. It is much better to have short training sessions given daily than long sessions of an hour or more once or twice a week.

Some dogs are naturally good swimmers and some unfortunately are not. Even with practice poor swimmers will never become as proficient as natural water dogs. Within breeds such as Spaniels, the variation in the individual's ability in water is vast. I have one English Springer who loves being in the water and is a fantastic 'duck dog'; I use him just like a Retriever during the season while flighting ducks on the river and ponds, and he loves it.

As the dog's handling improves, more dummies can be used.

In contrast, a few years ago I owned a Labrador bitch who, although she was adequate in other departments, was not a strong swimmer, despite Labradors being bred originally for water work. She would enter water readily and retrieve without any problem, as long as you didn't mind waiting ten minutes or so while she swam slowly out and slowly back. I eventually offered her to an American friend from Kansas, where they shoot mainly pheasants (upland shooting), and she seemed ideal for the job. Haynes came over to Scotland in late February to see the dog and to take her back to the USA. After demonstrating her on pheasants and rabbits, at which she excelled, Haynes wanted, quite rightly, to see her in water. We have a small lake up on the hills here, which, although reedy and boggy, is an excellent place to demonstrate a dog working in water. In February it is very, very cold. I threw a dummy as far as I could out into the middle of the lake and sent Bess to collect it. She immediately entered the water and slowly swam straight out towards the dummy. Unfortunately, as she neared the dummy, she stopped moving forward completely, and seemed to be stuck on something below the surface. We waited a few minutes (it seemed a lot longer at the time) in the hope that Bess would free herself or move or to do something, but she still seemed to be struggling. Haynes and I looked at each other, and he said, 'She's still your dog. I ain't paid you for her yet!' I had no choice but to strip off, wade through the bog and swim out to her. I have never felt cold like it in my life. Scotland in February is not the warmest place in the world, especially 1,200ft above sea level. I swam on as fast as I could until I could eventually reach out to catch hold of Bess, but just then she bobbed up,

Some Spaniels love the water.

swam to the dummy, picked it and headed back for shore, leaving me wallowing in the water like a stranded whale. When I eventually got back to dry land, Bess danced around me with the dummy still in her mouth, acting like this was great fun. Haynes was holding his camera but could not take any photos for laughing. Whether it was me splashing and causing waves that freed the dog (I think it was only some weeds she was tangled in), or the fact that Bess thought I was going to get to the dummy before her, which caused her to put in a bit more effort and free herself, I don't know. Once dried off and back in the house in front of a roar-

ing fire, I asked Haynes if he had taken any photos of the incident, and his reply was '*Wayoll a wows goin' ter, theyen a thowt, if ee drown out thar an me wid a load of pichas, stead of swimern awt ter git 'im, it'll look awfull baad!*'

I can laugh about it now but at the time I felt like drowning him and the dog. The moral of the story is that just because Spaniels are not supposed to be the best water dogs, it doesn't mean that none of them can swim well. By the same token Labradors, which as a breed are renowned for their ability in water, can also produce individuals who are terrible swimmers. Any

Throwing the distraction.

dog, given practice, can improve in water, and even a very poor swimmer will improve given time. The most important thing is never to do too much at any one time, and never try to force a dog into the water. This will only serve to worry him and may put him off water completely.

Once your Spaniel is handling well in and across water, this opens up a multitude of retrieving possibilities, only limited by your imagination and your access to lakes, rivers and ponds. The following are a few retrieves you might like to practise.

Exercise 1: Using an island.

Throw a dummy, unseen to the dog, onto the island. Fetch the dog and throw a marked retrieve parallel to the shore, then turn the dog to face the island and handle him out to pick the retrieve on the island. On his return, send him for the marked retrieve (this retrieve is known as a blind with a distraction).

Exercise 2: Using a pond close to a river.

It is very common to find duck ponds constructed in close proximity to rivers, and these are fantastic places to set up very difficult retrieves. Throw a dummy onto the pond unseen to the dog, then get the dog and from the far side of the river handle him out to cross the river and the piece of land between the river and the pond, and finally to enter the pond and retrieve the dummy. A distraction can be added, making it even more of a challenge.

Exercise 3: Teaching the Spaniel to enter water unseen by the handler.

This exercise is very useful as in many shooting situations, often due to steep banks at the water's edge,

Picking the blind retrieve on the island.

A challenging retrieve: a blind across a river and into a pond.

Teaching the dog not to swap retrieves.

the dog cannot see the handler and vice versa. It is very useful if the dog will take voice commands alone. Sit the dog at the water's edge and throw a dummy 25 metres or so into the water. Leaving the Spaniel sitting at the water's edge, climb the bank and walk away far enough that you can't see the dog and he can't see you. Once in position, blow the stop whistle (to get the dog's attention) and give the 'Go back' command; the dog should enter the water, swim out (into your sight) and retrieve the dummy. The next step is to throw two or three dummies into the water and pick them one at a time. The final challenge is to throw the dummy into the water unseen by the dog, and send him blind over the bank to the water's edge, then blow the stop whistle and give the 'Go back' command. He should enter the water immediately, swim out and retrieve the dummy. Again, as the dog becomes more adept with practice, a distraction can be added, making this retrieve very difficult.

Exercise 4: Throwing distractions when the dog is returning with a dummy.

It sometimes happens that a dog becomes distracted by someone shooting another bird while he is on his way back across water (or land) with a retrieve. The most common result is that the dog spits out his retrieve and heads for the other one or, worse, tries to retrieve both. Effective training can avoid the problem, and is very simple. Throw a dummy out into the water and send the dog to retrieve it. When he is on his way back, throw a dummy into the water, not too close to him to start with. If he diverts at all towards the splash of the new dummy, scold him and blow the recall whistle. As soon as he changes direction back towards you, give him praise and encourage him. Once he has learned to ignore the splash, you can throw the distractions slightly closer to him each time you carry out the exercise, and by throwing multiple dummies you teach the dog that swapping retrieves is not allowed.

CHAPTER 10

BEATING AND PICKING UP WITH THE SPANIEL

GROUSE DAYS

Beating is a great way to spend a day working your Spaniel in company with other like-minded individuals, some with dogs and some without. Although there is

a serious side to the job, as the Guns are paying a lot of money to shoot the game, there is always a laugh to be had (usually at someone's expense). Many people, who themselves don't actually shoot, find that 'a day at the beating' is a great way to spend a Saturday working their dog and getting paid for it. Normally it is not too difficult to find a shoot that will allow you to join the beating line, as good beaters with dogs are in high demand, especially those with well trained and well behaved Spaniels. When it becomes known amongst the local shoots that you own a handy Spaniel and are available, you will be asked to many more days and inevitably your diary will fill up.

For those who have never taken part in beating, I will explain how it works.

First, there is driven grouse, which starts on 12 August (the 'Glorious Twelfth') and goes through until December, although most shooting stops in early to mid-November as the weather later in the season on the hills can be very cold and wet. Grouse beating is very hard work, and a high degree of fitness is required, from both man and dog. It involves twenty to thirty individuals lined out over a half mile or more of heather ground using flags to chase the grouse towards the butts. These are stone or timber structures built for the Guns to stand behind to reduce the visibility from the grouse, which can be quite wary at times. There are normally between eight and ten guns and the butts will be in a line around 30 metres apart. The

Many people enjoy a day's beating.

Good beaters are in high demand.

Author's Comment

One very important point that I must mention is that Spaniels in particular can suffer from heat stroke, so when working dogs in August, you must be very aware of this, as within minutes they can collapse and die. I have seen it happen on three occasions and in one case the dog unfortunately died before the owner could get him off the hill to reach water.

If you suspect your dog is suffering from heat stroke, head for a stream or even a wet peat bog, but never just plunge the dog into the cold water as the shock could kill him. Instead, lie the dog down next to the water and splash water onto him with your hands or use your hat to pour water over him. This will cool him down quickly and he should recover within half an hour or so. When he comes round and is up on his feet, it is a good idea to give him something sweet to eat, such as a biscuit or similar, as this will boost his energy levels and help him recover. Very fit dogs do not seem to suffer so badly from the heat. In the three instances I have seen, all the dogs were slightly overweight having spent the summer months doing not very much. If you are planning on beating or picking up on grouse days, it is imperative to spend some time in July getting your dog fit and ready for a full day's work.

Shooting driven grouse.

Guns in grouse butts.

grouse, especially later in the season, can be quite wild so there is really no need to work your Spaniel early on in the drives, as flapping your flag is generally all it takes to flush a covey and send them towards the butts. However, on warm days grouse will sit very tight and this is when the Spaniel comes into his own. He should be hunted as normal in front of the handler under control and within working distance. As soon as the grouse flush, blow the stop whistle and wave your flag to send the covey in the correct direction. Many dogs, never having seen flags being flapped before, can be very nervous of them, and some training is required to allow the young dog to become accustomed to the noise and movement of the flag, and to teach him that it will do him no harm.

On many of the grouse moors in my area there is an abundance of mountain hares. These are fantastic

for teaching a Spaniel steadiness, whether by flushing them and watching them run off or by stopping the dog on hares that run up and down the beating line. He will soon regard them in the same light as sheep: not for chasing.

PARTRIDGE DAYS

Partridge days start on 1 September and in some ways driving partridges tends to be similar to driving grouse, although not so strenuous for handler and dog. Nowadays partridges tend to be driven from rushes and moorland edges, with the guns standing in the bottom of gulleys or behind stone dykes. Partridges will fly over the guns in large packs, making for some very sporting birds.

When beating at partridge days you will find that

Partridges fly over the guns in large packs.

they tend to run in front of the beating line, but as the beaters advance, waving their flags, they eventually rise and off they fly. It is important that you don't allow your dog to run forward when beating at partridge days, as this usually causes the birds to go back over the beaters' heads or to go out of the side of the drive, missing the guns completely. It is always advisable to hunt your Spaniel close to you, avoiding the possibility of him taking off in pursuit of the partridges. It is a great temptation for a young dog when he sees and smells all the birds running in front of him, the noise of the beaters and keepers, and the firing of guns all adding to his excitement. The handler's job is to keep the dog as calm as possible so that he remains obedient, thus avoiding the wrath of an irate gamekeeper ranting and raving because your dog 'ran in' and ruined the drive.

PHEASANT DAYS

The pheasant shooting season begins on 1 October and runs through until 1 February. In most cases driven days do not normally start seriously until November, and any pheasant shooting in October is usually 'walked up' or 'rough days'. This is mainly to give the pheasants a chance to mature, and for the ground cover and leaves on the trees to die back, which allows the pheasants, once flushed, to fly easily through the trees. On a typical pheasant driven day there will be between eight and fourteen beaters, plus a couple of 'stops' whose job it is to keep the pheasants in the woods until the guns are in place. As a beater your job is to go through the woods or game crops using your Spaniel to flush the pheasants out of their hiding places. You must keep in line with the rest of the beating team to avoid the possibility of the birds running back and away from the guns. Pheasants, especially after a few shoots, become expert at this.

An old gamekeeper friend of mine described pheasant rearing thus: 'The b****rs are suicidal until the day you want to shoot them. They then become better than Ray Mears at survival!'

One important point I would like to mention with regards to hunting your Spaniel in the beating line is that there will be many other dogs in the wood. It may

be that some of these are quite wild and not under the control of their owners; this can be a great temptation for your young dog. Under no circumstances should you allow him to join the 'pack' and run unchecked out of your sight. This will be the ruination of your dog as he will pick up every bad habit you can think of. I have seen dogs that, when the gamekeeper blows the horn or whistle to start the drive, immediately run off to the end of the wood and start picking up the pheasants that the guns are shooting, then drop them and chase after another. This is completely unacceptable and there is no place on a shoot for dogs like these.

Sometimes, if there is little or no ground cover in the woods in which you are flushing pheasants, your Spaniel will start to pull forward as he will smell the pheasants up ahead, and he can soon disappear out of your sight. It is much safer to bring him in and walk him to heel until you are in a suitable area of cover to carry on hunting.

When the drive is over, it may be that you are asked to retrieve some of the pheasants that have been shot, perhaps by a shooter who doesn't have a dog. Ask him approximately where the birds are, then go there and hunt your dog until he finds them and retrieves them to you. Do not try to handle the dog out to the area the gun has described, unless you have marked the fall of the pheasants yourself. When shooting, it is very difficult to mark game accurately, so the gun might think the bird landed 50 metres away when actually it is 100 metres further on. If you try to handle a novice dog out to the fall of a bird that isn't there, you are teaching him that you don't always know where the bird is. He might eventually find it 100 metres or so from the area you sent him to. The young Spaniel will then lose faith in you and may stop handling for you completely.

PICKING UP WITH YOUR SPANIEL (RETRIEVING GAME SHOT BY THE GUNS)

Driven Grouse

If you are lucky enough to be asked to pick up on a driven grouse day, you will be expected to sit in the heather up to 500 metres behind the line of butts,

Pickers-up are expected to sit down in the heather up to 500 metres behind the butts.

Grouse fly fast and low.

Jamie retrieving a runner.

shooters and flankers. You are there to mark down and pick birds which have been shot, wounded and carried on past the butts towards you, or even past you. Grouse fly very fast and low, so it would be extremely dangerous to be closer to the butts as there is a greater danger of being shot; as it is, safety glasses should always be worn during the drive. It is very bad practice – and will be frowned upon by the gamekeeper – to retrieve birds during the drives, as by moving around in plain view you can turn the grouse away from the butts. Even if it wasn't you who turned the coveys – maybe the wind is wrong, or some other factor kicks in – you will still get the blame. It is much better to sit low watching until the drive is over, then go and collect the wounded birds you have seen fall. This is the time when all your training and practice pays off, as you handle your Spaniel out to retrieve the birds which may have run, and it is a great opportunity to see the fruits of your labour and – with luck! – some fantastic dog work.

When you have picked all the grouse you saw fall, head slowly towards the butts, giving your dog plenty of time to cover as much ground as possible in order for him to pick any birds that you missed. Most of the grouse that fell around the butts will already have been picked by the keepers, beaters or guns, and they will tell you if they are short at any particular butt. It is then your job to hunt around the butts and pick anything that has been missed, while the guns and beaters head off for the next drive. There are normally four or five pickers-up on grouse days and it is good practice to discuss with the others which butts each individual covers, in this way avoiding birds being left on the ground unnecessarily – not least because the cost of shooting grouse can be upward of £180 per brace, so every single one counts! Once you have dropped off the contents of your game bag at the game cart, it is time to get back into the vehicles and set off to the next drive.

Hunting the dogs towards the butts.

Here they come!

Driven grouse days tend to be long; most gamekeepers want their helpers to be at the meet at around 8am and it is normally around 6pm before you leave the hill. Needless to say, a large lunchbox is required and also light waterproofs that can be carried in your game bag as the weather at higher altitudes can change in minutes from a beautiful sunny day to cold driving rain.

Driven Partridges (picking up)

Picking up at partridge days can be quite hectic, especially if the guns have come for a 'big day'. Unlike grouse, most of the partridges shot nowadays are reared, and very few wild partridge shoots, if any, still exist. It is possible therefore to rear and release large numbers of the birds, which are then flown across any suitable terrain, offering sporting shots for the guests. Bags on partridge days can be counted, on many shoots, in the hundreds, and I have heard of bags of over a thousand. On large days like these, you must never work your

young dog until he is exhausted. This can ruin the dog permanently; he will lose his drive and can even stop retrieving.

I find the best place to stand while picking up at partridge drives is directly between the guns, as the terrain is often not suitable for standing behind. By standing between the guns you will have a reasonable view of most of what is being shot and where it falls. The partridges that are shot dead and fall in the vicinity of the guns can be left; they are not going anywhere, and the beaters and keepers will pick them when the drive is over. Your job is to watch for the pricked, wounded birds and keep a mental note of their positions until the drive is finished. You can then walk there with your Spaniel and collect these partridges or, if the terrain is suitable, handle the dog out to pick them. In this way you will not work the dog to exhaustion and the shot birds are all in the game cart.

Once the beaters and guns have moved off to the next drive, it is a simple matter of hunting the Spaniel

The drive begins.

The safest place for pickers-up is between the line of guns.

around the areas where the guns were standing (pegs), as a last check that no shot birds have been left for the foxes and crows to devour!

Driven Pheasants (picking up)

Driven pheasant days give the guns, beaters and pickers-up great sport throughout the dark winter months. Most shoots start around 9.30am, and the last drive should be finished by 3.30pm. Especially up here in Scotland, the winter days are very short and time is of the essence to get all the drives done and the birds picked and hung up in the game larder, before cracking open the traditional bottle of whisky (and who are we to break with tradition!).

When using your Spaniel to pick up on pheasant days, it is quite acceptable to pick the birds during and after the drives as the birds are normally falling in woods or heavy cover where you will not cause any disturbance. It is always good practice, if any of the guns have dogs, to leave a few dead birds for them to pick when the drive is over. They are probably paying

A last check that no birds have been left.

a lot of money for their day and are quite entitled to have their own dogs pick their birds. Then it is a simple matter of sweeping the area when the guns and beaters move off just in case any of the birds have been missed. In many instances the guns will be lined out in short grass fields with the dead pheasants landing around them; again, these should be left for the guns and beaters to collect. It is much better to use these birds as a steadying exercise, not allowing your dog to pick them and making him sit quietly while the drive takes place. As you gain experience you will be able to anticipate the best places to stand for the various drives, allowing you to see exactly where the birds are falling and sending your dog to pick them.

It is a good idea to have a word with the gamekeeper before the first drive of the day and find out if there are any areas he does not want disturbed; there may be, for example, woods that are going to be driven later in the day. Any shot birds which land in these areas will be picked by the beaters as they move through the drive. To have a picker-up and his dog hunt a wood out before the drive takes place would be a disaster and an embarrassment for both the gamekeeper and the picker-up when there are no pheasants left for the guns to shoot.

Another bad practice I often see at shoots is pickers-up sending their dogs to retrieve birds as soon as they hit the ground, usually from 30 metres behind the guns in a flat grass field. This is completely the wrong thing to do, for two reasons. First, it serves absolutely no purpose, since dead birds are not going to move. If you send your dog for these birds time after time, he will very quickly start running in and no amount of training will ever stop him completely. Secondly, while he is running out to pick a bird, a gun may shoot another, whereupon the dog will spit out the bird he is retrieving and chase after the other ('swapping'). I have seen this happen time and time again during pheasant drives. In the end it is mayhem, with not one bird being retrieved and nobody knowing where any of the birds are that the dogs have dropped. This makes more work for you and the other pickers-up as the ground has to be swept to make sure that no birds are left behind, especially on

let days when the guns may be paying by the bird (and at upwards of £30 per bird, a lot of revenue can be lost to the estate or shooting syndicate). As a picker-up, you are paid to make sure there are no wounded or dead birds left unpicked. To know you have carried out the task to the best of your and your dog's ability can be very satisfying, and a job well done is much appreciated by the gamekeeper.

Welfare of Spaniels on Shoot Days

Spaniels use up a lot of energy in the course of a shoot day, whether beating or picking up, and if the weather is very bad they burn up even more just trying to keep warm. Long periods of inactivity while waiting for drives to start, or for the guns to get in position, exacerbates the problem. A dog should never be given his daily quota of food in the morning before a shoot. To expect a dog to work all day with a belly full of dog meal, or whatever you feed, would be ridiculous. However, some food should be given. I find that around a third of the dog's normal daily feed is adequate and provides enough 'fuel' to keep him going throughout the day without bagging him up and slowing him down. I like to feed my dogs again in the evening when they have been dried off, and I give them their normal daily feed. Even Spaniels that work three or four days a week will not lose weight during the shooting season if they are given an extra third portion every morning before setting off for the day's sport.

Lunch time on many shoots can be a long-drawn-out affair, especially on pheasant days, when the guns may have a three-course dinner and drinks, taking upwards of an hour and a half. Meanwhile the beaters, pickers-up and dogs are left waiting, sometimes in freezing conditions, for the afternoon drives to commence. In such circumstances, when lunch time arrives dry off the dogs and put them in a vehicle. One dog in the back of a pick-up will be very, very cold, but if there are lots of dogs they create their own heat and virtually turn the back of the pick-up into a sauna! As long as there is good ventilation, they will be very comfortable and ready for the afternoon's work.

CHAPTER 11

COMPETITION

GUNDOG TESTS AND TRIALS

Having trained and worked your Spaniel in the field, you may decide that you would like to enter a competition with your dog. These competitions are divided into two distinct types: Gundog Tests and Gundog Trials. They are breed specific, i.e. can be open to any variety of Spaniel or to Cocker Spaniels only. Both tests and trials are run by various gundog clubs spread throughout the country under the umbrella of the British Kennel Club, which polices the sport through the Kennel Club Field Trials Committee. Details of where and when tests or trials are taking place can be found by contacting the relevant Secretaries of your local Gundog Clubs, such as the South West Scotland Gundog Association, or National Clubs, such as the English Springer Spaniel Club of Great Britain.

Gundog Tests

Tests normally take place at weekends during the spring and summer months. Many are incorporated into Game Fairs, where the public can spectate. The idea behind tests is to replicate as closely as possible Spaniel Trials, but substituting game for canvas dummies. A variety of devices are used for replicating a Spaniel flushing game from cover (usually involving feral or homing pigeons being released from a trap), either manually or electronically. Two Spaniels and handlers will be required by the judge to hunt up a particular piece of ground at the same time, normally getting the opportunity for each of them to flush a pigeon, whereupon the dog is expected to sit to flush while a shot from a blank or starting pistol is fired. The judge will then ask the handler to send his dog to pick various dummies, which

may be blind retrieves, marked retrieves, doubles or blind retrieves with a distraction. The other handler and dog are expected to wait quietly for their turn to make a retrieve. In most tests there will be at least one retrieve out of or across water.

The judge then scores the dog on its hunting and subsequent retrieving ability, usually out of a maximum of 100 points. Spaniel Tests are split into three groups, depending on the dogs' age and experience:

- Puppy Class (dogs up to one year old)
- Novice Class (dogs which have not won a test or trial)
- Open Class (this is open for any dog or handler to enter and the standard can be very high)

Points will be lost for various misdemeanours and faults, including poor delivery, failing to stop when the handler blows the stop whistle, failing to sit to flush or shot, and not covering its ground properly during its hunt. Tests are a fantastic method of socializing young dogs and getting them used to the competition environment. Many experienced trainers run their pupils in puppy tests for this reason alone.

The best piece of advice I would give the prospective trialler is to go to as many tests as possible and watch closely the dogs that regularly win. Most gundog triallers and judges are very approachable and you should take every opportunity to seek their advice by having a word with them when the competition is over, perhaps to find out why a particular dog was marked down or another one got full marks. All this information will help you decide whether your Spaniel is up to the task of running firstly in tests and ultimately in trials. If your Spaniel has any eliminating or major faults, it is a waste of time and money entering tests or trials as the fault is guaranteed to show up under the pressure of competition.

Some eliminating faults include barking or whining at any time; hard mouth (damaging game); running in (retrieving without being sent); chasing un-shot game; failing to retrieve; and missing game on your beat.

It is very difficult for anyone to train their first gundog up to the standard required to be successful in tests or trials, but it is not impossible and it can be done. Even if your dog is not suitable, you still have a first-class shooting companion – and also an excellent reason to buy another pup and start again! With the experience and knowledge you have gained through training your first Spaniel, you will not make the same mistakes again.

Gundog Trials

Gundog Trials and Spaniel Trials on the whole are much more serious affairs than tests, and can also be quite expensive to enter and compete in. Entry fees can be around £50, and when you add in your fuel expenses and maybe overnight accommodation if the trial is a long distance away, you may not see much change from £200. Trialling is a sport and, like any other sport, it costs money to participate. Many people are happy to pay their money and enjoy their sport.

The first step to entering the trial circuit is to join some of the gundog clubs that run trials in your chosen area. Details of these can be obtained from the British Kennel Club or found online. Again, spend time going along to spectate at the trials and get to know some of the competitors, organizers and judges, who will be able to give you much valuable advice and generally point you in the right direction.

If, after a few days' spectating at trials, you still feel that you and your dog are up to competing, the next step is to enter a few novice trials. These are open to dogs who have not won a trial, but do not be fooled by the word 'novice': there will be many very experienced handlers competing and probably some top-quality dogs, and the standard can be very high. Most trials are over-subscribed, as the maximum number of competitors allowed to run is sixteen. The remaining

Dogs, handlers, judges and guns lined out for a novice Cocker Spaniel stake.

Golden Nectar gets a nice find and flush.

entrants will be reserves in numerical order as they appear in the draw. You may not get a run in every trial you enter, so it is best to enter as many as possible, in this way maximizing the probability of being successful in the draw. The draw normally takes place in a public area with the Gundog Club Secretary and a few committee members present. This ensures that the draw is fair and unbiased.

A few days after the draw, you will receive the results either by post or email. If you have been successful, your number will be between one and sixteen, and you are about to run in your first trial. Believe me, your first trial can be a very nerve-racking experience, right up to the moment when the judge tells you to take off your leash and hunt your dog in a certain direction. I find that as soon as the dog is out working and my concentration is totally on him, all nervousness disappears. From then on, until the end of your run, it's just you and your dog, and putting him in a position to produce game to be shot.

When you receive the results of the draw, you will also receive directions and timings for the meet. Always turn up at least half an hour early, as this gives you a chance to exercise your dog and allow him to clean himself and loosen up after his journey. Offer him a drink of water before putting him back in your vehicle. The next job is to find the Club Secretary and introduce yourself. You will be given an armband with your number on, and a running card listing the names and numbers of all the competitors and the details of their dogs.

Before the trial starts, the Secretary will normally make a short speech, introducing the guns, judges and host, and giving the competitors and any spectators instructions of where and where not to go. Once he has declared the trial started, you are under the direction of the judges (usually two, one on the left of the line and the other on the right). There will normally be four or six guns lined out ready to kill any game that is flushed.

When it is your turn, your number will be called. Introduce yourself to the judge you are running under, shake hands and follow his directions. He will tell you where he wants you to hunt and what direction to take. It is then up to you to produce game, making sure your dog covers the ground of its beat properly as, if any game is missed or flushes behind the dog on an upwind beat, you will be discarded from the trial and your debut is over for the day.

If you are lucky, your dog will find a rabbit or pheasant, flush it and sit immediately to flush, whereupon the game is shot and killed. The judge may then ask you to retrieve it, or he may offer it to the other judge for his dog and handler to pick, especially if the other dog has had a long run without a retrieve, or for various other reasons. If you are asked to retrieve the game, it should be done smartly and efficiently with a minimum of handling and noise. The bird or rabbit must then be handed to the judge, who will check for damage caused by the dog ('hard mouth'). Finally he will tell you to continue hunting or to put your dog on the leash if you have had a reasonable time to hunt and produce game. Later in the day you may be called again to run under the other judge ('second run'), where you will hopefully have another successful hunt and produce more game to be shot and retrieved.

When all the competitors have had two runs, the judges will get together and go through their notes, discussing the various dogs' hunting style, drive and retrieves by placing them in order. The top dogs may then be taken back in for a 'run-off', to decide first, second, third and fourth places, or, if two dogs are very close, to give one the opportunity to outshine the other and produce a clear winner.

As with all sports, discussion among the competitors and spectators is prolific, everyone having differing opinions and views of their own and other people's efforts during their time 'under the judges'. Criticizing their own dogs and other people's dogs is all par for the course and is quite acceptable, but criticizing the judges' decisions is not and must be discouraged at the highest level for the good of the sport.

There are three important reasons for this. First, the judges have been asked to judge by the organizing club because of their experience, their knowledge of dogs and game, and their impartiality. Judges are unpaid and many take time off from work to perform this service. Questioning their decisions is an insult to their credibility. Secondly, the judges are the only people present at a trial who have seen all the dogs hunting and all the retrieves being carried out. It stands to reason, therefore, that they are the only ones who can make the correct informed decision. Lastly, trials in general are not fair. There is nothing fair about them. However hard the judges try to give every competitor a similar run, the very nature of the sport does not allow for this.

Golden Nectar, handled by Fran Ardley and eventual winner of the stake, gets the retrieve.

Judges deliberate to decide the results.

Let me explain. One competitor is given an excellent piece of cover to hunt, where he can show off his dog's prowess and produce game easily, perhaps a pheasant that is shot and lands dead 30 metres from the handler. The judge then asks him to retrieve the bird (which the dog has marked), and the dog retrieves it efficiently to hand, without any handling – top marks awarded. The next competitor unfortunately runs out of the good cover and his beat is in forest brash or even short grass, where it is very difficult to show off a dog's hunting ability to any advantage. Suddenly there is a shot fired from the end of the line: a snipe has been shot 100 metres or so away, unseen to the dog and handler. The judge says to retrieve it, which will not be an easy task. My point is trialling can never be a level playing field, and your bad luck today is another competitor's good luck. Tomorrow it might be your turn for providence to smile on you. The most important factor in winning trials is that you run a good, well trained dog, and are able to take advantage of that 'luck' when it comes to you. It is not the judge's fault if your beat is poor and produces

no game; he has little choice in deciding where the trial is taking place. Whether you had a good run or bad, whether you are still in the trial or out, it is common courtesy to thank the judge and shake his hand – and try again another day.

If your young Spaniel is well trained, has no faults and covers the ground stylishly and efficiently, you will eventually win your first trial. This is the best feeling in the world! All the training and practice, all the getting out of bed at 3.30am to travel hundreds of miles to compete, all the times you lost trials because your dog missed a rabbit or failed on a retrieve – it is all in the past. You are now hooked and could not stop trialling even if you wanted to. I have run in HPR Trials, Spaniel Trials and Retriever Trials with a modest amount of success in them all, and believe me when I say that it is far easier to start trialling than it is to stop!

Once you have won a novice trial with a particular dog, you are then qualified to enter him in Open trials. These are run along exactly the same lines as novice trials, but your dog will be expected to carry out more difficult retrieves, to hunt methodically within the proper distance without continual whistle commands, and generally be more 'finished'. The standard of these Open trials is very high among both dogs and handlers. Winning an Open trial goes towards the much-coveted title of Field Trial Champion.

Successful field triallers are dedicated to training their dogs and running them in competitions. Many have spent most of their lives honing the skills required to produce good trial dogs time and time again. If you are going to compete successfully at this level, it stands to reason that you are going to have to sacrifice a large amount of your time to the training and practice necessary to be competitive. Many of the trials fall on weekdays, meaning holidays are used up, and in many cases trialling results in family vacations and a social life becoming things of the past. If you are still keen to have a try, I have listed here a few useful tips and general advice on training and preparing your Spaniel specifically for trials:

1. Never allow your Spaniel to hunt too far from you; keep it tight and cover the ground systematically.
2. Always take note of the wind direction and use it to your advantage.
3. When training, never hunt the dog for long periods, allowing him to tire. Ideally a five- or six-minute hunt producing one head of game followed by a retrieve or two is perfect.
4. Encourage the dog to sit to flush and shot automatically, removing the need for the stop whistle.
5. Teach the dog to sit quietly in front of you, and also at a distance, while other dogs are retrieving.
6. Never take a prospective trial dog in the beating line at shoots; in general, beaters walk too fast and this does not allow the dog time to cover its beat properly, which encourages him to develop a poor pattern when hunting.
7. If you are picking up at shoots, never give the dog too many retrieves, especially not too many runners. Everything should be done in moderation.

A very happy Andy Plat with his newly made up Field Trial Champion (Boots), FTCH Rollafields Redbud at Naxshivan.

8. Never allow your dog to chase rabbits around in standing bracken. This type of cover is not useful in Spaniel training: the handler can't see the dog, the dog can't see the handler, and the rabbits tend to run around out of sight, not allowing for a shot.
9. Rushes are perfect for training Spaniels, although you must practise in all types of cover, including gorse, nettles, game crops, etc., as you may be asked to hunt through any type of vegetation during a trial.
10. Make sure your dog will retrieve snipe and woodcock; it is not uncommon for some dogs to refuse.
11. Practise in the company of other triallers whenever possible, allowing your dog to become accustomed to hunting with a brace mate (simulating trial conditions).
12. Whenever possible, have an assistant shoot the game, allowing you to focus on the dog.
13. If your dog moves even a foot or two after flushing a rabbit or pheasant, scold him instantly and return him to the point of flush.

In the following section of this book, I have asked a few of the most consistent and successful field triallers of all breeds in the country to give one piece of advice to potential triallers, which, in their opinion, is the most important factor to success.

John Halsted: runs Retrievers and has won the British Retriever Championship on many occasions with many different dogs.

Good Breeding

'I think the best piece of advice I could give to someone who is considering becoming involved in Gundog Trialling is to buy from the best breeding stock available in order to have the best chance of producing a suitable dog.'

Iain Openshaw: runs Cocker Spaniels, English Springer Spaniels and Retrievers. He has won both the Cocker Championship and the Springer Championship on numerous occasions.

Basics

'The single most important factor in consistently turning out successful trial dogs is to make sure that the basics are done properly. If the basics are not thoroughly taught to the young dog, it cannot and will not be competitive at any level.'

Jim O'Niel: runs English Springers and has made up many Field Trial Champions.

Patience

'I think it is important to let the puppy be a puppy and not try to start training him too early; far too many young dogs are ruined through novice trainers trying to teach the pup before it is mentally and physically mature. The dog will let you know when it is ready to be trained.'

Billy Steel Snr: runs Retrievers and has made up many, many Field Trial Champions over the years, and has come very close to winning the championship on numerous occasions.

Repetition

'Teaching the basics thoroughly and repeatedly all through the dog's training and trialling career. Never consider your dog fully trained, as there is always room for improvement.'

David Lisset: runs English Springer Spaniels, Cocker Spaniels and Retrievers. David trains and handles dogs professionally for the Duke of Buccleuch and has won the Spaniel Championship numerous times.

Communication

'Communication is probably the single most important thing to consider when training dogs – be they gundogs, sheepdogs or working dogs. Using the whistle in conjunction with body language and verbal sounds to communicate to the dog at the right time whether we are happy and pleased with him, or annoyed and displeased with him, for carrying out a specific action. In short, the dog must clearly know when he has done well, or when he has done wrong.'

Eddie Scott: runs English Springers and Cocker Spaniels. Eddie has won Spaniel Championships on various occasions and made up many Field Trial Champions.

Encourage Natural Hunting Ability

'I think it is very important to allow young dogs to develop their hunting ability naturally, starting at a very young age by encouraging them to explore their new world of scent, game and cover. By not inhibiting this instinct to hunt in any way, we allow the young Spaniel to develop its full potential.'

Andy Platt: runs Cocker Spaniels and English Springers (as well as Lurchers, Terriers and Hounds!). Andy has made up many Field Trial Champions.

Assess your Dog Honestly

'Assess your young dog through play training and always try to spend more time improving his weak points. It is too tempting if a young dog is good at hunting to do more of this, but it is important, if this is the case, to spend more time getting the retrieving right. A Spaniel of good breeding will be likely to be a natural hunter so get the handling done first, and then work on his hunting pattern. Never mix the two in one lesson.'

Billy Steel Jnr: runs Retrievers. Billy has made up many Field Trial Champions, has won the British Championship and has run dogs professionally.

Preparation and Marking

'Prepare thoroughly for a trial; know exactly what will be expected of you and your dog on the day. Mark everything that is shot accurately, remembering precisely where the game falls. This can mean the difference between winning a trial and being disqualified.'

This is excellent advice from some of the best gundog trainers in the United Kingdom, and indeed the world, as here in the UK we set the standard and are respected by gundog people not only in Europe but also in the Americas and more recently in Eastern Europe, where gundog trials are becoming increasingly popular.

Whether you are training your Spaniel as a shooting companion, a beating or picking-up dog or intend one day to run in a gundog trial, I sincerely hope this book has been of some benefit to you, as well as an enjoyable read. Dog training on the whole tends to be more of an art than a trade, and some things work for some people and not for others. I have tried to describe honestly, and as simply as possible, how I train Spaniels. It is not rocket science – it is simple, it is rewarding and most importantly it is fun, both for you and your dog.

Happy Hunting!

INDEX